"The Matthewses are the First Family of Football and Bruce is their patriarch, one of just over three hundred to have a bronzed bust in Canton, Ohio, as the greatest of all time. All of us can learn from his faithful journey of commitment, character, courage, and compassion—what it takes to have a Hall of Fame family and Hall of Fame life."

—**David Baker**, president, Pro Football Hall of Fame

"I had the honor of being a teammate with Bruce for ten years. He was the most talented and versatile offensive lineman I played with during my twenty-three-year career. The Matthews family to me is the 'First Family' of NFL football! It is truly amazing the talent in this one family tree. This story needs to be told, and I'm happy the sports world will get to learn more about this truly amazing family lineage. I slept better the night before games knowing that Bruce was lining up next to me!"

—**Warren Moon**, NFL quarterback, inductee in the Pro Football Hall of Fame

"In my twenty-three years of coaching in the NFL, Bruce Matthews was one of the most competitive yet humble teammates I ever had the privilege to coach. He was a warrior in the trenches on the gridiron and has always been a warrior for Christ. Join him in his family journey as he takes you inside the locker room and the life of a Hall of Fame player. Button your chin straps! . . . You're going to love this!"

—**Les Steckel**, veteran NFL coach, former president/CEO Fellowship of Christian Athletes

"This is an honest and revealing story about the life of one of the greatest to ever play in the NFL. It is a fascinating 'behind the scenes' look at the NFL, as well as a personal story of overcoming life's challenging obstacles. Whether you are a sports fan or n~~~ Bruce's journey as a father, a husband, and a

T0042826

have been a close friend of the Matthews family for over thirty years and continue to be inspired by the love and support that they have for each other and the faith that guides them all."

—**Mike Munchak**, Hall of Fame former professional American football player, offensive line coach for the Pittsburgh Steelers

"While reading this book I could feel Bruce's spirit and energy, which is raw and inspirational. Bruce embodies all of the qualities of what and who a man is. His strong core values and beliefs jump off of each page. Those same qualities permeated in our locker room where Bruce was a wise, loving, faith-filled, persistent, and tenacious 'granddaddy' role model. I knew without a doubt that for the seven of my eight years as an Oiler/Titan, I could always count on Bruce Matthews to be there, no matter what, even when injured. And I'm extremely grateful."

—**Eddie George**, NFL running back, Heisman trophy winner, inductee in the College Football Hall of Fame

"Bruce Matthews is a winner as an NFL player, a husband, a father, and a man of God. His new book, which tells the amazing story of the Matthews family, is a winner too. If you're looking for inspiration to be better in every aspect of your life, you need to read *Inside the NFL's First Family*."

—**Tim Brown**, NFL Hall of Fame wide receiver and author of *The Making of a Man*

"*Inside the NFL's First Family* provides extraordinary insight into Bruce Matthews's journey from childhood to the Pro Football Hall of Fame. The Matthews family has embodied greatness on the field for three generations. *First Family* shows what an important role their faith in God has played in helping them become leaders and role models who set a standard that transcends the sport that has made them so successful."

—**John McClain**, NFL writer for the *Houston Chronicle* and member of the Pro Football Hall of Fame committee

INSIDE
THE NFL'S
FIRST FAMILY

MY LIFE OF FOOTBALL,
FAITH, AND FATHERHOOD

BRUCE MATTHEWS
WITH JAMES LUND

HOWARD BOOKS
AN IMPRINT OF SIMON & SCHUSTER, INC.

New York   London   Toronto   Sydney   New Delhi

Howard Books
An Imprint of Simon & Schuster, Inc.
1230 Avenue of the Americas
New York, NY 10020

Copyright © 2017 by Bruce Matthews

Literary Representation by Premiere Authors Literary Agency

First Howard Books paperback edition August 2017

HOWARD and colophon are trademarks of Simon & Schuster, Inc.

For information about special discounts for bulk purchases, please contact Simon & Schuster Special Sales at 1-866-506-1949 or business@simonandschuster.com.

The Simon & Schuster Speakers Bureau can bring authors to your live event. For more information or to book an event, contact the Simon & Schuster Speakers Bureau at 1-866-248-3049 or visit our website at www.simonspeakers.com.

Manufactured in the United States of America

10 9 8 7 6 5 4 3 2 1

Library of Congress Cataloging-in-Publication Data

Names: Matthews, Bruce, 1961- author. | Lund, James L., co-author.
Title: Inside the NFL's first family : my life of football, faith, and fatherhood / Bruce Matthews, with James Lund.
Description: First Howard Books hardcover edition. | New York : Howard Books, [2017]
Identifiers: LCCN 2016027820| ISBN 9781501144783 (Hardcover) | ISBN 9781501144790 (Ebook) | ISBN 9781501145339 (Tradepaper)
Subjects: LCSH: Matthews, Bruce, 1961- | Football players—United States—Biography. | Football coaches—United States—Biography. | Houston Oilers (Football team)—History. | Tennessee Oilers (Football team)—History. | Tennessee Titans (Football team)—History.
Classification: LCC GV939.M2963 A3 2017 | DDC 796.33092 [B] —dc23
LC record available at https://lccn.loc.gov/2016027820

ISBN 978-1-5011-4478-3
ISBN 978-1-5011-4533-9 (pbk)
ISBN 978-1-5011-4479-0 (ebook)

To my mom, Daisy Crowson Matthews,
for being the heart and soul of my family and for offering
amazing love and encouragement every day of her life

FOREWORD

THE AVERAGE PROFESSIONAL FOOTBALL CAREER IS a brief one—just shy of seven years, according to the NFL, and half that according to the NFL Players Association. I was fortunate enough to play thirteen seasons in the NFL, and I played every game in the season six times in those thirteen years.

Bruce Matthews played nineteen seasons as an offensive lineman in the NFL—nearly three times longer than the average player's career. Only once in those nineteen seasons did he not play every game. For the final fourteen seasons of his glorious tenure, Bruce not only played every game, but started every game he played. In all, from 1983 through 2001, Bruce played 296 NFL games and started 292 of them; by the time he retired, no position player had ever played more.

This is an incredible accomplishment, made even more so by the fact that Bruce played every position along the line during his nearly two decades of NFL excellence, and was never less than exceptional at any position and in any game. If there was any question regarding his sustained greatness, the following will quickly silence that debate. He was a nine-time first-team All-Pro, and went to fourteen straight Pro Bowls—nine at guard and five at center. Only one other man has ever made fourteen straight Pro Bowls, and that's Merlin Olsen, the Hall of Fame defensive tackle who spent his entire career with the Los Angeles Rams.

Two hundred ninety-six NFL games; figure an average of sixty plays per game, and that's on the low end. So that's 17,760 NFL plays over the course of a career, and that's just the games. Unlike today, players practiced in full pads, with hitting several times a week during the season. Pick a number of plays per practice and multiply that over Bruce's nineteen-year career.

Those are the numbers, and that's a lot of football, all of it performed at an exceptionally high level. But that shouldn't be surprising, considering the family heritage Bruce brought to the field: His father, Clay, played four NFL seasons during the 1950s, and Bruce was preceded into the NFL by his older brother, Clay Jr.

Desire and the demand for achievement are the chords that sound throughout Bruce's career, but over and above that is the call of family. I had the great honor of sharing the field with Bruce six times during my career. I was flattered when Bruce asked me to write this foreword.

That he would ask me to write for him was quite an honor to bestow on an old opponent. But then I considered that, despite our roles as opponents, we also shared a very particular bond beyond competition.

Football runs in the Matthews' family, just as it now does in mine. I've already mentioned Bruce's father and older brother, and I can well imagine the enormous pride Bruce felt as he followed in their footsteps, determined to live up to their standards. Reading about how Bruce and Clay felt the two dozen times they faced one another, I'm glad I never had that issue. I'd like to think I was one of Bruce's most challenging opponents, but I know—as has been the case in our family on the infrequent Sundays my two sons line up against each other—that Bruce's toughest opponent was his older brother Clay.

Bruce and I have been blessed to see our sons play at the game's highest level. He's seen sons Kevin and Jake play in the NFL, as I've seen my two oldest, Chris and Kyle, join me as an NFL pro. And after all, what does a man want but to carve a path for his family and leave a legacy for his children? Certainly Bruce and all the Matthews have done that. Football to me is about family, and throughout the NFL's history there have been many legacy players: brothers, sons, nephews. With all due respect to those other families, through multiple generations over multiple decades, the Matthews could well be the first family of football.

When my middle son Kyle was headed to the draft, there were two players I referred to him over and over as players to emulate, both of them Hall of Famers: former Oilers player Mike Munchak and, of course, Bruce. They were the absolute best. I saw a lot of those two great players in Kyle from a physical standpoint, but to Kyle these were just two faceless names until one of his pre-draft trips took him to Tennessee where Mike was the head coach and Bruce was the offensive line coach. I was excited for Kyle to meet them, and he was excited to get the opportunity to meet these two men who I cited over and over for their greatness.

You could make the case that, because of his adaptability, Bruce is the most versatile, dominant player who has ever played offensive line. He essentially carved out his own category of excellence. In this salary-cap era, I cannot imagine what a player with his unique skill set—the potential to be a Pro Bowler at any offensive line position—would be worth.

But in the end, the greatest compliment one player can give another is also the simplest. Bruce played the game the way it is supposed to be played: with athleticism, with strength, and most of all, with respect. I hope you enjoy the story he lays out in the following pages. If he writes as well as he played, you're in for a Hall of Fame treat.

—*Howie Long*

PROLOGUE

IN 1983, ON THE DAY BEFORE Halloween, thousands of fans dressed in orange and brown filed into Cleveland Municipal Stadium for the Browns' National Football League contest against the Houston Oilers. Cleveland fans were known to be rabid, but for most followers of the NFL this was far from the game of the week. The Browns had lost three straight and were 4–4. The Oilers were still seeking their first victory after eight tries. Injuries had sidelined Cleveland's quarterback, former MVP Brian Sipe, and Houston's star running back, Earl Campbell. It was the kind of game most media commentators passed over when they previewed the upcoming week.

But for me, the story was different. I could not have been more pumped up. You see, I was the starting right guard for the Oilers.

My excitement wasn't because I thought I had a chance to finally earn my first professional victory. And it wasn't because I was a starstruck rookie, though I still had moments when I couldn't believe I'd actually arrived on football's biggest stage.

No, I was thrilled for only one reason—for my first time as a pro, I was about to do battle with my big brother.

Not many families can say they've had more than one member

play professional football, but that fall I'd become the third Matthews to enter the NFL fray. My dad, Clay Matthews, started what's become a family tradition when he took the field as an offensive tackle for the San Francisco 49ers back in 1950. It was the first of four NFL seasons, which were interrupted by two years of military service. My older brother, Clay Jr., raised our family's NFL profile when he joined the Browns as a first-round draft pick in 1978, quickly becoming a star linebacker and launching what would become an amazing career. By the time I arrived, I just hoped to uphold the family name.

Actually, I intended to do a bit more than that. If there's anything that rivals the love and pride the Matthews family feel for each other, it's our competitive spirit. We *live* to compete.

I'd looked up to and competed against Clay—or "Bruz" as I've called him since my older sister referred to him as her "bruzzer" as a child—for as long as I could remember. Football, basketball, baseball, Ping-Pong, video games, it didn't matter. We were always going at it. The problem for me was that Bruz was an excellent athlete and five years older, and no way was he going to let me win. We might be playing two-on-two "knee football" on the carpet in our house with my brothers Brad and Ray. It was all good fun with easy tackles, unless the game got close. Then Bruz imposed his will physically and made sure his side won. Or it might be one of our ferocious one-on-one hoops battles in our driveway. Bruz typically gave me room to shoot early in games. But if it was game point and I had the ball, his defense clamped down. Trying to drive against Bruz was like hitting a steel post. It was all I could do to get off a half-court hook shot.

We played a lot of basketball as I grew up, but from elementary school through junior high through high school, I never won a single game of hoops against my brother. He just refused to lose.

On that Sunday in Cleveland, however, I figured it was time to start a new tradition. I admired my brother, but I was ready for some revenge.

The buildup had started earlier that week. On Wednesday, I sat with the offense in a meeting room not far from our home field, Houston's Astrodome. We were going over the game plan and figuring out how to neutralize the Browns' playmakers. "Bruce's brother is obviously the outstanding player on their defense," said Kay Dalton, our offensive coordinator. "We've got to take care of him." I loved hearing that. I hoped no one was watching me right then because I had a big smile on my face.

When the projector went on and showed film of the Browns in action, I had trouble focusing. My instinct was to watch Bruz. I saw him make tackles and break up plays all over the field. Then I thought, *Oh yeah, I've got to watch who I'm playing against.* It took me a few years to learn to put aside the fan side of me.

I was definitely struggling with my inner fan the day of the game. I'd been rooting for my brother and the Browns ever since he'd joined them. Cleveland's stadium was massive, with seating for eighty-thousand people. Nearly seventy thousand showed up to watch our game. This was in the days before team jerseys were common attire for home fans, yet when I scanned the huge crowd I was surprised and moved by how many Clay Matthews number fifty-seven uniforms filled the arena. Also in the crowd, sitting together, were my wife, Carrie, and Bruz's wife, Leslie. Standing on that field for the first time as a player and surveying the scene was an experience I'd never forget.

Cleveland's stadium sat right next to Lake Erie and could attract some nasty weather, but that afternoon it was a reasonable forty-six degrees at kickoff. On the game's opening drive, the Browns advanced to our nineteen-yard line. Then our defense held and the Browns kicked a field goal.

In the huddle before our first offensive play, our quarterback, Gifford Nielsen, called for a short pass. After we broke the huddle and I stepped toward the line of scrimmage, I was still struggling with my emotions. *Oh man, that's my brother over there. There's Chip Banks and Tom Cousineau. I know all these guys.* Then I shook my head and got into my three-point stance between center David Carter and tackle Harvey Salem. It was time for business.

After a couple of first downs, our opening drive stalled. But our second drive was more successful, as Nielsen hit Mike Renfro with a nineteen-yard pass to the end zone for a touchdown.

We still led 7–3 when we got the ball back for our third drive of the game, now early in the second quarter. One of the plays in vogue then was the counter trey, which John Riggins and the Washington Redskins had employed so successfully during the previous Super Bowl. The counter trey was a misdirection running play. Our running back would take a step to the right, as though the play were going that way. Meanwhile, the right tackle and I pulled out of our normal position and sprinted left to block opponents on the other side of the field. After his fake, our running back followed behind us.

We had the counter trey in our game plan against the Browns. It was a big deal for me because my assignment on the play was to take out Bruz. I couldn't wait. When we'd talked about it earlier, Kay Dalton said to me, "You can't take it easy on your brother."

"Heck, no," I said. "I'm going to light him up."

Just before that third drive, Dalton had pulled me aside on the sideline. "We're going to run the counter trey at your brother."

All right, I thought. *Here we go. After all those years of Bruz being the big brother and having his way with me, I'm getting my payback right here.*

I was so keyed up I barely remember Nielsen calling the play— "Jab thirty-seven"—in the huddle. "Relax," I told myself. "You've run this play before. Treat him like any other player. Just make sure you show him there's a new kid in town."

The play began just the way it was supposed to. Our running back feinted right while Harvey Salem and I pulled left. Bruz saw what was happening from his position at right outside linebacker and moved in, just as I expected. I ran at him full bore, aiming my forehead at his temple. I braced for what I knew would be a violent collision. Our helmets would crash together like a couple of butting rams. I was going for a knockout block that would open a huge hole for the running back behind me.

Except that isn't what happened. Bruz sidestepped me like a hummingbird dodging a charging bull. I whiffed. Instead of me laying my brother out, Bruz stuffed our runner, Donnie Craft, after a minimal gain.

I don't think Bruz even knew it was me trying to block him until after the play was over. He figured it out, though, when he looked back and saw me slowly rising from the ground. I'd done a faceplant into the turf. Back in the day, the so-called grass at Cleveland Municipal Stadium was so sparse, the groundskeepers spray-painted everything green to make it look like grass. I was getting up while trying to remove green sand from my face mask.

"Hey," Bruz said when he saw me, a grin on his face. "Open your eyes next time."

That was my introduction to playing against my brother in the NFL.

It got worse. We led 19–13 in the third quarter, but the Browns kicked a pair of field goals in the fourth quarter to tie us, the last one with forty-nine seconds left. The game went to overtime. In the extra period, Cleveland safety Mike Whitwell intercepted one of our passes and returned it to our twenty-yard line.

Bruz must have been feeling pretty good at that point, because he ran over to me after the play and bumped me with his shoulder. It wasn't that hard a hit, but it was enough to draw the attention of one of the officials. He reached for the yellow flag in his back pocket, apparently to call a penalty on Bruz.

"No, no," Bruz said while rushing over to the referee. "He's my brother. It's all right."

I have no doubt that the officials calling our game had developed as much respect for Bruz by that time as the players. The referee kept the flag in his pocket. On the next play, Browns running back Boyce Green ran twenty yards over right tackle for a touchdown. The game was over.

Was I disappointed about losing and about whiffing against my brother? You'd better believe it. But at the same time, I felt so thankful to be on that field that I couldn't get too upset. If I had to lose that day, at least someone in the Matthews family walked away a winner.

You could say that's the Matthews family in a nutshell. We love to take each other on and will show no mercy no matter what the contest—yet we're always rooting for each other and delighted to see each other succeed.

Our family has been blessed with many more opportunities to square off against each other since that game in Cleveland. Bruz's career lasted nineteen seasons and included four Pro Bowl trips and three seasons with All-Pro honors. He's still the Browns' franchise record holder for career tackles, sacks, and forced fumbles. I was fortunate enough to also play nineteen seasons, start 229 consecutive regular-season games (most ever for an offensive lineman), and earn fourteen Pro Bowl and seven All-Pro honors, which led to my induction into the NFL Hall of Fame in 2007.

It's the next generation of the Matthews family that's making waves now, however. Bruz's son Clay III has starred for seven years as a linebacker for the Green Bay Packers. At this writing he's a six-time Pro Bowler and has been a first-team All-Pro. He's also been named NFL Defensive Player of the Year and owns a Super Bowl ring. His brother, Casey, played linebacker for four years with the Philadelphia Eagles before moving to the Minnesota Vikings. My son, Kevin, meanwhile, is a center who's spent five seasons in the NFL with the Titan and Panther organizations. His younger brother, Jake, has been a starting tackle for two years with the Atlanta Falcons. And my son Mikey spent training camp with the Browns in the 2016 season as a rookie center.

I guess that's why some people describe us as the NFL's First Family and why *Sports Illustrated* recently put us at the top of their list of best all-time football families. Are there more Matthews NFL players on the way? It's certainly possible. Time will tell.

I'm proud of each of these guys—father, brother, nephews, sons—but I'm just as proud of the wives, siblings, sons, and daughters in my family and in the extended Matthews family who aren't NFL players.

In his or her own way, each is a success and has contributed so much to this world. I love them all.

That's a hint at what this book is about. It will tell my story, the journey of a big, shy kid who became an NFL Hall of Famer. But it is also an inside look at the Matthews family and the qualities that have allowed us to flourish in the NFL and elsewhere. Please don't get me wrong: I don't claim to have life all figured out and I've made plenty of mistakes along the way. But by God's grace, I've been blessed with a wonderful career in football, a faith that sustains me, and the best family a man could ask for.

I invite you to keep reading. I hope that the following pages will be entertaining. Even more, I hope they will provide a few insights that will help you on *your* journey.

Ready? All right, let's go.

1

TOUGH BUT FAIR

Competition is the spice of sports;
but if you make spice the whole meal you'll be sick.
GEORGE LEONARD

PEOPLE SOMETIMES ASK ME, "HOW DO you guys do it? What's the secret that enables your family to keep turning out NFL players?"

There are many answers to that question. One of them is that we've been blessed with good genes and bodies that can take a pounding. But there's definitely more to it than that. It's a story that begins more than a century ago, back to at least 1889. That's when my grandfather, Howard Lynn "Matty" Matthews, was born. He got his start in Jeffersonville, Ohio, but spent most of his life in Charleston, South Carolina. That's also where he met and married my grandmother, Elsa "Booty" Bargmann.

Matty began his athletic career in baseball, playing in the minor leagues from 1911 to 1915, primarily in the South Atlantic or "Sally" League. He never earned a spot on a Major League roster yet he made his mark in other ways. Matty was fast, which led to a position switch from catcher to outfield soon after he reported to his first team in Macon, Georgia.

According to a newspaper clipping from those days, the Detroit Tigers and Boston Red Sox were in Macon for an exhibition game that first spring. The best-known name in the big leagues during the early 1900s was Ty Cobb, the "Georgia Peach" and Detroit Tigers outfielder who would become one of the original inductees into the Baseball Hall of Fame. Cobb was famous for his hitting and nasty disposition, but also for his fleet feet. He stole 892 bases during his career, which at the time was the all-time record.

A newspaperman came up with the idea of a footrace featuring my grandfather, Cobb, and another player. The contest was a sprint from home plate to first. I can imagine onlookers placing more than a few wagers before those competitors squared off. If they bet on Cobb or the other player, they lost their money. Matty beat them by three yards. Even then, it seems, the Matthews family hated to lose.

When America entered World War I, Matty joined the army. They introduced him to the sport of boxing and it grew into one of his life's passions. In 1926, he joined the staff of the Citadel, the military college in Charleston. He coached boxing, baseball, and track and field there, but it was boxing that built his reputation. He taught the sweet science to Citadel cadets for nearly three decades and coached a number of champions. Just a few years ago I spoke at an event in Charleston. After I was finished, some of the elderly locals spoke to me. They told me about taking boxing lessons from my grandfather, saying he was tough but fair. I thought that was pretty cool.

My grandfather passed on his athletic genes to my dad and my dad's two brothers, but Matty also gave them a major dose of his toughness and will to win. He had all three of his boys boxing before they entered elementary school.

Dad grew up in Charleston and continued to hone his boxing skills. He was a two-time heavyweight Golden Gloves champion. The only fight he ever lost was his first—his mother made his trunks and, in the first round, the elastic popped. Dad was trying to fight with one hand while pulling up his trunks with the other. During the fight, he yelled at his mom, "Look what you've done!"

Boxing wasn't my dad's only sporting interest, however. He went to college at Georgia Tech, joined the wrestling team, and became the Southeastern Amateur Athletic Union heavyweight champ. He was eventually elected to the Georgia Tech Athletic Hall of Fame. He was also a college swimmer and diver.

But competing in the ring, on the mat, and in the pool wasn't enough challenge for my dad. He also decided to test himself on the gridiron. At Charleston High, he went out for the school team and was a standout on the offensive and defensive line. He continued with football in college.

Those years were part of a golden age for Georgia Tech football. In 1947, my dad's first season with the varsity, legendary coach Bobby Dodd was in just his third year with the Yellow Jackets. The team won nine of its first ten games, losing only to Alabama before knocking off Kansas, 20–14, in the Orange Bowl. They were nearly as successful the next two seasons, finishing with a 7–3 record both years.

Dad enjoyed plenty of athletic success in college but, in those days, professional sports were not nearly as lucrative as today. They weren't the answer for most young men who wanted to make a decent living.

Dad graduated with a degree in industrial engineering and planned to use it.

Then he got a call from a representative of the San Francisco 49ers, a team that had just joined the NFL, saying the draft was over and they wanted him on their team. The league draft wasn't a media sensation back then. Dad never did hear when he'd been chosen. Many years later, when I was with the Oilers, I was in the training room and picked up a *Los Angeles Rams Media Guide*. I'd always been interested in the history of the game, so I looked up the Rams' annual draft results. Suddenly, I saw a familiar name. I was so excited that I called my father that night.

"Hey Dad," I said, "I picked up a media guide today and found out when you were drafted!"

"Oh?" he said. "When was it? The first round?"

"No," I said. "The twenty-fifth round. You were the last pick of the Rams. Then they traded you to the 49ers."

Dad obviously wasn't at the top of the 49ers' prospect list, yet the chance to compete and test himself against the best was too appealing to pass up. He decided to report to the 49ers for the 1950 season. Dad made the team, earned a salary of about $6,000—decent money back then—and played in all twelve games for San Francisco as a right tackle on offense and a tackle and end on defense. He recovered two fumbles, recorded an interception, and even returned one kickoff.

The 49ers wanted him back for 1951, but Dad had a new challenge in mind. By then the United States was involved in the Korean War and Dad wanted to be part of it. He volunteered to become a paratrooper and was sent to Fort Bragg in Fayetteville, North Carolina, for training. The leaders at Fort Bragg pushed their men hard, trying to weed out those who might quit on the battlefield. My dad was one of those who lasted. He eventually made twenty-one jumps as a member of the U.S. Army's 82nd Airborne Division, though he never saw action in Korea. Dad's brothers, my uncles, showed the same kind of determination and desire to test themselves. Lynn, his older brother, graduated from the United States Naval Academy and eventually commanded a nuclear submarine. Dale, Dad's younger brother, became an ace jet pilot in both the Korean and Vietnam wars.

Jumping out of airplanes wasn't the only thing on my dad's mind at Fort Bragg, though. It was while he was in Fayetteville that he was introduced to a vivacious woman named Daisy Crowson. She was, in my dad's words, "Gorgeous, blonde, with green eyes and a nice figure. A sweet lady." They married in 1953.

When the U.S. signed the armistice ending the Korean conflict, Dad returned to civilian life and the NFL. After three more years with the 49ers, the team traded him to Philadelphia. By this time my parents had a daughter, Kristy, who was born in 1954, and Clay, who was born in 1956. Dad was already making more money in the off-season than he was as a player. He decided it was time to exchange his uniform for a suit and tie. It was the right decision financially, because he would soon have more mouths to feed. My twin brothers, Brad and Ray, were born in 1959. I joined the Matthews family on August 8, 1961.

Little did I know what I was getting into.

◆   ◆   ◆

One of my biggest impressions of my early years, really of my whole childhood, was of packing up and driving to a new home. Part of my dad's job at the time was shutting down unproductive factories for Scovill Fasteners, a company that's still around to this day. The result was that we moved a lot.

When I was born, we lived in Raleigh, North Carolina. We moved to nearby Clinton when I was one or two, then we were off to Wisconsin, Michigan, and North Carolina again before we moved across the country to Arcadia, California, for my final three years of grade school. All the moving meant I didn't keep friends for too long. Maybe that's why our family is so close-knit. We learned to depend on each other because, so often, we were all we had.

Not that we sat around complaining about it. We were too busy discovering new ways to compete against each other. That need to test oneself, so important to my father and grandfather, definitely passed on to me and my siblings. Bruz, Brad, Ray, and I played all the usual outdoor sports and relished each battle (Kristy was usually more interested in horses than in messing around with her brothers). We also turned to standards of the day such as electric football or tabletop hockey. We sat on the floor, hunched over, and twisted the rods that controlled those metal hockey players until our backs were sore. But it was great fun.

When we got tired of traditional contests, we turned to more creative pursuits. Baseball was one game we decided we could play anywhere. First it was indoors, pitching a Nerf ball against a batter with a rolled-up newspaper. Then it was in the basement, hurling darts at a dart board while a batter wielded a two-by-four—you had a hit if you got the dart to stick in the "bat." Nobody was maimed, but we did have a few brushback pitches.

After we moved to California, our competitions became even

more inventive. Bruz and I created a baseball game that we played in our backyard pool. The pitcher floated on the surface, facedown, and dropped or spun the "ball"—a circular steel plug, less than three inches in diameter—toward home plate, which was actually the drain at the bottom of the pool, six feet down. Also at the pool bottom was the batter, who recorded a base hit by getting the plug to rest on the back of his hand.

We played that one often. In theory, the pitcher wasn't supposed to delay in delivering his pitch, because the longer he waited, the less air the batter had, and the more likely he was to fumble his "swing" or make a bad decision. That was the theory, but my memory is that Bruz used that tactic against me often.

I don't remember doing the same back to him, of course. But it's possible my brother's memory of those times might be a little different.

When I look back on those competitions with my brothers, I wonder how we survived. Part of it was knowing when to stop (or Mom or Dad making us stop). The other part must have been God watching over us.

Dangerous or not, I loved every minute of it. Something about contending for a victory, even if the reward was just bragging rights that lasted only until the next game, made me feel alive. I couldn't get enough of it. Naturally, I loved recess at school. Kickball, softball, punch ball—whatever was going on, I was in the middle of it.

It was during fourth grade that I also got into Little League baseball. I was a catcher and pitcher. I was pretty good too, a consistent line drive hitter. Though I couldn't run fast, I was quick to get after the ball and make the throw to second base. I started dreaming of becoming a Major League catcher. I was a big kid, weighing 125 pounds. I was so big, in fact, that I sometimes hindered the umpires. I remember one adult ump saying quietly to me after he called a ball, "Sorry, that might have been a strike. I couldn't see over you."

My baseball success led me to try out for a Junior All-American football team. It turned out, however, that they had a weight limit. I was twenty-five pounds too heavy. Bruz wouldn't let me forget that one. He kept telling me, "You're the first Matthews to ever get cut from a team."

My desire to compete usually brought out the best in me, but there have been a few occasions when it *got* the best of me. One of those times came a few years later, when I was sixteen. I'd never done much boxing. Dad didn't insist on it the way his father did with him, though Dad did teach me how to throw a jab and protect myself. Then one day I got in the mood to throw a few punches.

"Hey," I said to my best friend, Dave "Sam" Samarzich, "let's spar a little."

We started messing around in our driveway. It was supposed to be just a bit of fun, but pretty soon I was peppering Dave in the mouth with jabs. The problem was that Dave wore braces, the old-school kind with lots of metal. Dave started getting ticked off, and with good reason. His mouth was all bloody.

My dad happened to come home from work right then. He was not happy about what he saw.

"You're going to take advantage of someone like that?" he said to me. "That's crap."

Dad walked into the garage and returned a few seconds later. He tossed a pair of boxing gloves in my direction. "All right, tough guy," he said. "Put the gloves on."

I knew I was in trouble. "Dad, I'm sorry," I said. But it was too late.

At that time I was probably six foot three and 225 pounds, the same height as and heavier than my dad. But it didn't really matter how big I was. I wouldn't have lasted a single round against him if he'd been trying to knock me out. To his credit, he only wanted to make a point. He hit me with just a couple of jabs and it was like the old Rocky movies, with my head snapping back like a yo-yo on a string. All I could think was, *Oh, my gosh, I do not ever want to tangle with my dad.*

Dad taught me a lesson that day—competition is great, but there's a line that you don't cross. To put it another way, be tough but fair.

Despite that driveway confrontation with my dad, my desire to compete and win actually intensified as I got older. It always showed up during my continuing competitions with Bruz. When I was at the University of Southern California, he and his family lived near the campus. During his off-season, I would drive over and we might start with a fierce Ping-Pong war. Then we'd sit on his couch and play video games on one of the old Intellivision consoles. There was plenty of taunting and smack talk, including at least a few imitations of the Jets' Mark Gastineau doing a sack dance. Those battles could go for hours, until two, three, or four in the morning—however long it took for me to win.

I certainly drew on my competitive nature while playing football for USC and when I reached the NFL. It was a major motivating factor in my drive to excel and defeat my opponent whenever I stepped onto the field. Yet the most fun I had competing continued to be the games and battles of skill and wills with Bruz. That was probably because we learned where to draw the line with each other. I still remember the day we figured it out.

● ● ●

It was May 1983. I was about to graduate from college and start my pro football career, while Bruz was already a five-year NFL veteran. Our family had gathered for a picnic at a friend's backyard in California's High Desert. Either Bruz or I spotted a couple pairs of boxing gloves lying in the grass, so of course we had to put them on. We were just joking around, flicking little jabs at each other, when—at least as I remember it—Bruz suddenly popped me. I don't mean a knockout punch or anything like that, but enough that it stung a bit and upped the ante. Naturally, the competitor in me had to respond. I jabbed him back, this time a little harder. The next punch from Bruz came back harder still.

We both would have said nothing was going on, but I'm sure if the people around had been paying attention, they would have said, "Dang, those guys are fightin'!"

Pretty soon we were in a clinch that for a moment felt more like a stand-up wrestling match. Then the lightbulb went on for both of us and we separated.

"Hey man, what are you doing?" I said. "Why'd you start getting serious?"

"What do you mean?" Bruz said. "You started punching me!"

I had a scratch from my temple down to my cheek. We were fortunate that neither of us suffered anything worse. I was embarrassed that we'd let things get out of hand. I'm sure Bruz felt the same way.

From that point on, Bruz and I dialed our battles down a notch.

For one thing, the stakes were higher—an injury could have put either of our careers in jeopardy. But more than that, speaking at least for myself, I didn't want my intense desire to win to somehow create tension or put any distance between us as brothers. We still did and do love to challenge each other, but now it's more about the joy of competing and being together than the need to score a victory.

For example, a few years after I got to the NFL, we started a weekly "sports day" during our off-season. This consisted of getting up at five in the morning, joining our buddy, Bob Queen, at Denny's for a Grand Slam breakfast, and proceeding in the predawn darkness to a public golf course. Golf was so popular in Southern California that it was next to impossible to secure a tee time, so we got a jump on the crowd. When the first rays of sunlight crept over the hills, we were already at the first tee, ready with our drivers. We had the course to ourselves, as it wouldn't open for another half hour.

Our matches on the links were pretty even though none of us was a stellar player. After eighteen holes, we'd head over to a bowling alley for five or ten games. I have to admit that Bob usually won those contests. That took most of the afternoon, but Bruz and I both played on city league softball teams, so we always had a game or two in the evening. In later years, we added tennis to the equation.

You've probably got the idea by now—I truly love competing, and Bruz is my favorite opponent. But it's taken me quite a few years to put that insatiable desire to win in its proper place. In college and later in the NFL, my competitive spirit was a huge source of strength. Sometimes, though, it was also a weakness. Once in a while I found myself saying or doing something I wasn't proud of—cussing out a referee or losing my temper and making an unnecessarily vicious block.

You might be reading this and thinking about your own competitive nature. Believe me, I'm not suggesting that you should be ashamed of it or give it up. I just believe that when it crops up, it needs to be managed. As I look back on my football career today, I remember players who possessed that healthy, competitive drive. You could see why they were a notch above others, why they stood out. They demonstrated it was possible to be a great player without being a jerk. I feel that I also got there, eventually. It just took me a little longer than I'd like to admit.

Today, I'm grateful that my temperament includes that inner fire. It's an important part of who I am. But I'm also thankful that, though I still slip up on occasion, I've learned how to channel it in healthy ways. It's better for me and for the people around me.

Even Bruz might agree with that.

2

DOWN BUT NOT OUT

In this world you will have trouble.
But take heart! I have overcome the world.

JOHN 16:33

IN 1970, THE YEAR WE MOVED to Arcadia, my dad was named head of a regional facility operated by a motion-picture equipment manufacturer. Among other items, Bell & Howell made the projectors that our teachers used to show us films in class.

In a lot of ways, Arcadia was the perfect place for a kid going into fourth grade. The fast-growing Pasadena suburb offered plenty of sunshine, sports, and California dreamin'. The city sat at the base of the San Gabriel Mountains and featured a number of beautiful spots. Some of them attracted the entertainment industry—in a few years, the opening for the popular TV show, *Fantasy Island*, would be filmed there.

Most of my fantasies centered on baseball. As a catcher, I loved being part of the action on every pitch and thinking about how I'd react to what the batter did. I dreamed of being the next Johnny Bench and playing in the Major Leagues. Since Arcadia was just north of Los Angeles, most people in the area were big Dodgers fans. However, because of my dad's days as a 49er, my team was the San Francisco Giants. I rooted for guys like Willie Mays, Willie McCovey, Juan Marichal, Bobby Bonds, and Dick Dietz.

Not that I limited myself to baseball. During football season, either my brothers or the neighborhood kids and I tossed the pigskin in the backyard. I pretended to be NFL kicker Tom Dempsey and booted the ball over our clothesline. During basketball season, we shot hoops. Just about any time, we enjoyed swimming in our backyard pool or riding our bikes—the old kind with a banana seat, chopper handlebars in front, and a sissy bar in back. One morning, before school, I tried to ride up a wall and ended up landing on my head. That was my first concussion.

Arcadia was a great place for a young boy to grow up, but after three years there, my dad was promoted to corporate vice president. We needed to move again so Dad could be near Bell & Howell headquarters. Our new destination was Kenilworth, Illinois, fifteen miles north of downtown Chicago.

Actually, I was excited about the move when I first heard about it. I knew we would have a big house within walking distance of Lake Michigan, which sounded fun. In Arcadia I shared a bedroom with my three brothers—we had two sets of bunk beds—but in Kenilworth I'd get a room of my own. That sounded great too. I put out of my mind that every family move had been tough for me initially. I was naturally shy, so making friends at a new school and adjusting to new routines was always a challenge.

This time it was worse.

It hit me on the first day at our new home. It was August. We arrived in the late afternoon after flying more than two thousand miles. The house was a two-story Tudor, red brick in front and a basement underneath. I ran into the empty house—the furniture hadn't arrived yet—and up to the second-floor bedroom that would be mine. The back of the room featured a bank of windows overlooking a large backyard with tall trees and lots of open grass. *Hey*, I thought, *this is pretty cool.*

But in the next instant, reality set in. All my friends and the familiarity of Arcadia were gone. Once again, I was starting over with unknown classmates, teachers, and procedures. I wouldn't even share a room with the people I was closest to, my brothers. I would be alone.

A cloud of dread suddenly hung over me. *Oh, my gosh, I don't care how cool this is. I want to go back. I don't want to deal with this.*

Unfortunately, I wasn't feeling just momentary anxiety. The burden that seemed to weigh me down wouldn't go away. Once the school year started, I struggled to get up every morning. I didn't want to talk to people in class. On Sundays, the thought of going back to school the next day was unbearable.

In hindsight, I recognize that any kid facing the junior high school years in new surroundings is ripe for some anxiety issues. But at the time, I couldn't seem to get over them. Just getting through the day was exhausting.

Football practice for the seventh- and eighth-grade Kenilworth Rebels started soon after we moved in. I looked forward to competing in organized tackle football for the first time and hoped it would lift my spirits, but after that first afternoon of pushups, sit-ups, up-downs, bear crawls, and every other drill that a football coach could imagine, my anxiety took over. "I don't want to be here," I said under my breath as I walked off the field. "What's the fun of being sore and stiff and out of breath and getting yelled at by coaches? I don't want to play football." Not the most auspicious start for a guy who would play the game for the next twenty-nine years.

In time, however, playing for the Rebels did become a kind of escape from my low feelings. Even though I was a seventh grader, I started as a stand-up defensive end and began to enjoy being an important part of the defense. It wasn't just the games, either. I actually looked forward to practice and the chance to work on fundamentals, get better, and compete against my teammates. The football field began feeling like my home away from home. It helped that we won almost every game we played.

Those good feelings lasted until the seventh contest of the season, a home game. It was almost halftime. I was running upfield to take on the fullback's block when a guy from the other team came at me. I anticipated him hitting me up high, but he suddenly went low—he might have tripped—and hit me square in the left leg, just below my knee.

The next thing I remember was being on my back on the grass, my leg pointed at a weird angle, concerned faces surrounding me. I felt a combination of numbness and pain: not surprising, since I'd broken my tibia and fibula. Ironically, despite all the games that would follow, it was the worst football injury I ever suffered. A field hockey game was underway nearby, so the medical team at our game borrowed a field hockey stick and used it to fashion a splint. I was loaded into a station wagon and transported to Chicago's Northwestern Memorial Hospital.

One of my first thoughts wasn't about me or my team, but about Bruz. He was a senior at New Trier East High School in nearby Winnetka and the star of the team as a fullback and middle linebacker. The Indians were undefeated, and I loved watching them play on Saturday afternoons. *Man*, I thought as I lay in the station wagon, *I hope this doesn't make me miss any of Bruz's games.*

It did, of course. I was in the hospital for two weeks. Even though my season was over when I was released on crutches and wearing a hip cast, I still enjoyed football and could still attend the rest of my brother's games. New Trier East remained undefeated the rest of the season and was state champion. Bruz was team MVP. I was as proud as a little brother could be.

● ● ●

My parents saw that I was struggling with the move to Illinois and adjusting to our new life. Several times my dad sat me down for pep talks. "Come out swinging" was one phrase I remember. I know he meant well, but I can't say that it helped me much. What I did learn from those conversations was that I wasn't the only one having trouble adjusting.

My mom, Daisy, was a Southern belle: blonde, beautiful, and tan, with big hair and an even bigger personality. Mom was outgoing and always seemed to draw people's attention. When we lived in Arcadia, she joined the crowd trying to become a contestant on the game show *The Price Is Right*. Sure enough, she got on. She won

Skyway luggage, an air-hockey game, and a pool table before she was through.

Mom had a way of making an impression. A few years ago, I was reminded of that during an NFL Hall of Fame promotional event in Cleveland the weekend before the NFL draft. It was the year my son Jake was up for selection. I was on a bus and noticed an older gentleman in the seat behind me reading a booklet about the top draft candidates. I asked if I could borrow his booklet, flipped to the page with Jake's bio, and said, "Hey, this kid right here, you should pay attention to him. He's a can't-miss NFL prospect."

The gentleman looked at the name, then up at me, and put it together. "You're Clay's boy!" he said. I hadn't recognized him, so I was thrilled to discover I was talking with Hugh McElhenny, the great running back for the 49ers in the fifties, a Hall of Famer, and a teammate of my dad.

"Your dad and Daisy, they were such great people," he said. "Your mom, Daisy—she was country, but whoo, she was good lookin'!" Sixty years later, Hugh McElhenny still remembered her.

Mom also got the attention of my friends in Little League. After I was born, she and Dad gave me the nicknames "Beatie Butterball" and "Beatus" (no, I did not mention that to my NFL teammates). When I played Little League baseball, Mom always came to our games. Whenever I came up to bat, she yelled in her best Southern drawl, "Come on, Beatus!" Of course the rest of the guys on the team started calling me Beatus. But that was Mom. She was there to root on one of her kids and wasn't afraid to let everyone know it.

After we moved to Kenilworth, though, I noticed that Mom sometimes went to her room to lie down and get away from everything. It wasn't like her to withdraw. She was usually so engaged with whatever was going on. But I didn't think much about it. Then, during one of my conversations with Dad about feeling down, he said, "Yeah, your mother has those same feelings. She struggles with it too."

The truth is that my mom was dealing with depression. She'd had bouts of it before the move to Kenilworth and continued to battle it off and on for the rest of her life. I never spoke to her about it. As a twelve-year-old, I had little understanding of what depression was or what was going on with her. I just knew that she wasn't feeling well.

I have to give my dad credit. As important as the new position at Bell & Howell was for his career, he recognized what was happening with Mom and me and decided something had to be done. One day not long after Thanksgiving, he gathered my mom and all five of us kids and announced that most of the family would be moving back to California at the end of the school semester. "I'm staying here for now," he said, "and Clay will finish his senior year here, but the rest of you guys are going back to Arcadia to help your mom out."

"Cool!" was my immediate response. I'd begun to get a little more comfortable with Kenilworth, but the idea of returning to sunny Southern California was more than all right with me. Just knowing that we were going back lifted my spirits. In mid-January, we moved into a new house, about three miles from our old one in Arcadia. It was a good change for Mom. Her depression lessened, though she still had her hard days. For me, it was like I'd never left. I was soon hanging out with old friends again and playing Little

League baseball. It was tougher on Clay, who had to complete high school without the support of much of his family, and on Dad, who flew to California almost every Friday and back to Illinois on Sunday night.

Now that I was back in my comfort zone, I figured my battles with feeling low were over. I figured wrong.

On the tree of health issues, depression is a unique branch. There are so many ways that our brain chemistry can be disrupted. Unlike a broken leg, you can't see depression, so it's difficult to identify and treat. People often don't understand or sympathize with someone who's dealing with it. But it's definitely an issue for many people.

I grew up in a football family and have spent my whole life in the macho culture of football. I used to think about problems like depression, *Well, you just suck it up until it goes away.* Now I realize that, sometimes, it doesn't go away. I once believed that real men take care of their problems on their own. But the truth is, real men are not afraid to ask for help. Many athletes have talked openly about their depression issues, including the NFL's Terry Bradshaw, the NBA's Jerry West, and major league baseball's Zack Greinke, who for years has taken medication for social anxiety disorder.

We all struggle with one thing or another. If you're dealing with depression or any other illness, you don't have to put up a front. Talking to others about potential solutions is always a smart move. I'm not ashamed to say that I have struggled with occasional depression throughout my life. Right after holidays are one of the times when it can still hit me, though it's not as severe as it used to be, and nothing compared to what some people go through. I have tried a low-level prescription of depression medication, and though I've never been one to tout drugs as the answer, I understand and appreciate that they are exactly what some people need.

I have a lot of compassion and respect for people who are dealing with depression and similar maladies. From my mom's experience and my own, I understand how hard it can be to just get through the day, let alone accomplish great things. In my case, the understanding and support of my family has made a huge difference.

3

"YOU'RE A MATTHEWS"

Life is a succession of lessons
which must be lived to be understood.
RALPH WALDO EMERSON

IT WAS SPRING 1974. A TV show called *Happy Days* had debuted in January, and plaid pants were "in." Since Dad was still commuting from Illinois, however, he was often "out"—as in out of town. As great as it was being back in Arcadia, it wasn't quite the same on the days when Dad wasn't around.

When Dad was with us, I felt like I was in the presence of the coolest dude around. Maybe that's why I looked forward to Fridays so much after the move to Arcadia. Sometime during the evening on Friday, a driver would pick up Dad at the airport and bring him home. It's not that we all had this big reunion when he walked in the door. In fact, he and Mom would often go out to dinner soon after he arrived. But just knowing that he was back and that they were together was reassuring. When Dad was home, everything just felt right.

As usual, I played Little League baseball that spring and summer. We played twice a week, once on a weekday and once on Saturday. Since Dad couldn't make the weekday games, it was always special for me knowing that he was in the stands on those Saturdays.

Unlike my mom, Dad didn't holler during the games. Other than a comment such as "You played well," he didn't say much after the games either. Even though he'd acquired a ton of sports know-how over the years, he rarely offered advice unless his kids asked for it. During baseball season, we did often go into the backyard to play catch. Though I was primarily a catcher, I also spent time on the mound as a pitcher. If I wanted to work on my technique, he'd grab his glove and catch for me for as long as I wanted to throw.

I do remember a time after one of my sixth-grade basketball games, though, that he couldn't help himself. He'd watched me have limited success against my opponent, a kid named Alex Iles, who went on to become a famous trombonist. Alex and I were about the same height but I was thicker, heavier, and stronger. "Bruce, you're too nice out there," Dad said. "You've got to be physical. You're bigger than he is. Use your size advantage on him. Lean on him. Outwork him. Out-hustle him."

At first I didn't know what he was talking about it. *What do you mean, I'm too nice? How can that be?*

But Dad's words got my attention. I was pumped up for the next game. *All right,* I thought. *I'll show him.* As soon as I got into the lineup, I played with intensity. I was physical. I hustled. I aimed to "impose my will." Sure enough, I had a great game.

Dang, I thought. *He was right.*

Dad also encouraged me in football. He was helpful whenever I asked a question, yet always gave me space to enjoy the sport on my terms. Maybe that was because Dad had other priorities in mind for his kids. He definitely was intentional about the life lessons he wanted to pass on. By word and, especially, by example, Dad showed what being a Matthews was about.

I learned that one of the qualities of a Matthews is persistence—the ability to fight through obstacles. Dad still loves to tell the story about how, as a senior at Georgia Tech, he competed in the state Golden Gloves heavyweight finals at ten o'clock one night, then wrestled for the Southeastern Conference heavyweight title at ten the next morning. He won both championships.

Another favorite story comes from his NFL days. "We were playing the Chicago Bears in 1954," he'll say, "and I was at linebacker, covering Bill McColl, their big end. I was watching the quarterback, and McColl got inside me. I ran right into the goalpost. Wrapped my arms around it. I was out cold! But I stayed in the game, calling the defensive signals. In those days, we had a trainer nicknamed Anak the Faith Healer. I'd say, 'I'm hurting.' And he'd say, 'Tape an aspirin to it.'"

By the time I entered eighth grade, I already knew plenty about Dad's persistence. He was tough and he never quit. But the idea that this philosophy applied to every member of the family didn't fully sink in until after I went out for basketball that year. I'd been playing on teams since grade school and had enjoyed it, but after three or four games that season I started to lose my enthusiasm. Maybe it was because I wasn't contributing that much and was figuring out that basketball wasn't really my game. Maybe it was the ultrashort gym shorts we all had to wear. Whatever the reason, I didn't have the same passion for the sport.

I was standing in the kitchen one day with my dad when we started talking about the team. And out of my mouth came the words: "Yeah, maybe I won't keep playing basketball."

I meant to keep it casual. Really, I was just floating an idea. But as soon as I said it, I wished I hadn't. I knew what was coming next. Dad's head snapped around and his eyes flashed.

"Hey, you're a Matthews. You start something, you finish it. You don't quit."

That was the end of the conversation. Dad hadn't raised his voice and I'm sure he quickly forgot about it. But I never did. Though I already understood it, it was that moment in the kitchen when an important part of the Matthews family code was fully branded into my consciousness.

You're a Matthews. You start something, you finish it. You don't quit.

Needless to say, I finished the basketball season.

That philosophy stayed with me during my nineteen years as an NFL player and is what I believe as a husband and father. I credit this to my dad. He didn't just preach it, he talked and lived the Matthews code, and he made sure his children understood what it meant.

I can't count the number of times during my football career when I felt pushed to the limit and wanted a break. *Oh, my gosh*, I'd think, *I am dying. I am so tired out here.* Then that stubborn, competitive, never-give-up Matthews trait would kick in. *But hey, if I'm tired, those guys on defense must be in even worse shape than I am. So bring it on.* My attitude as a player was, "You may get the best of me now, but if you give me enough time, I'm going to find a way to beat you. This is a marathon, not a sprint." I was sure I could outlast the other guy.

That approach applied just as much when I was at home. For

instance, I had a simple rule for my kids: No going to PG-13 movies until you're actually thirteen. As you can imagine, it wasn't a popular decree. So many times, I heard about friends whose parents allowed them to go to R-rated movies while my kids couldn't even see a PG-13. There were times when I thought, *Ah, maybe it's all right. Why do I even bother with this? What really is the big deal?* It's not like I enjoyed seeing my kids unhappy or feeling left out.

But in the next instant, I'd remember that just like a football game, parenting is a marathon not a sprint. I'd set that standard because I didn't want to expose my children too soon to certain language and images. I wasn't going to give up on my beliefs just because it was easier in the short term. I needed to persevere and stay the course.

To be honest, I prefer taking the easy path. Yet somehow over the years I've been able—most of the time—to push through my fatigue and doubts and do what needs to be done. I may not actually hear Dad's voice in my head when I feel tempted to give up or give in, but to this day, my foundation is based on those words he delivered back in our kitchen when I was thirteen years old.

You're a Matthews. You start something, you finish it. You don't quit.

●　　●　　●

There were other elements to what I now call the Matthews code that Dad impressed on me and my siblings. I remember weekend nights when just he and I would sit in our family room in Arcadia. It had a floor-to-ceiling glass panel with a view of the backyard pool. The evening would begin with us watching television together. Then Dad would start telling stories. Somehow, the night always seemed to end with a lesson or life point.

If the topic was sports, Dad would say how important it was to volunteer to do what needed doing, to always be the first guy in line. He talked about hustle. He encouraged me to do what the coach told me to do. "Your coach may not have the best strategy," Dad would say, "but if you and the rest of the players are all on the same page, you'll have a great opportunity to succeed." Dad's words always left me feeling encouraged.

The biggest lesson of all had to do with integrity and doing the right thing.

"If you look a guy in the eye, shake his hand, and tell him you're going to do something," Dad would say, "or if you say, 'You can count on me,' make sure you follow through. Nothing's more important than your integrity." He explained that it applied in marriage, in the workplace, or wherever I happened to be.

I understood what he meant. My commitments didn't need to depend on a signed contract. Once I gave my word, that was it.

I've talked about that with my kids. So many student-athletes today will commit to a college, for example, then change their mind a few weeks or even days later. I didn't want to see that with my family. "Look," I told them, "once you say you're going to do something, then you're committed. So think long and hard about your decisions. You've got to carry yourself with integrity."

Not that I've always demonstrated great integrity myself . . .

When I started college, Dad encouraged me to pursue an engineering degree. I'd always been good at math and science, but I knew it would be a stretch to combine football and engineering study. That first semester was a challenge. So, before one physics test, I decided I needed a little extra help. I wrote down some equations and answers on a piece of Scotch tape and stuck it to the inside of my down vest.

It was ridiculous. I knew it was wrong when I did it. But somehow I allowed myself to believe it was all right, that I was taking on a heavy load and deserved a break.

The irony is that during the test, I never looked at the tape. I'd attached the tape too low inside my vest—it would have been obvious if I'd tried to read what I'd written there. Even if I could have read it without being seen, I felt so guilty about it that I don't know that I would have anyway.

Oh well, I thought as I prepared to hand in my test. *I didn't need those answers anyway. No harm done.*

Or so I thought.

My vest must have flipped open a little too far. The professor at the front of the room pointed at me and said, "Come here." When I got up to him, he said, "What have you got inside your jacket there?"

I'd been caught and there was nothing I could say. I got a D on the test and in the class, and was fortunate it wasn't an F. The whole incident was just embarrassing—and a great reminder to me that no matter how appealing it might be to put my integrity on hold, it would only lead to trouble.

After all the conversations with my dad growing up, I haven't really needed to talk about those issues with him anymore. I already know what he'll say and I know in my heart what I need to do. Not that the temptation to compromise my integrity has gone away. Every year when I sit down to do my income taxes, the enticement is there. I almost have to laugh when the idea of fudging some figures pops into my head. *This is stupid*, I'll think. *Why are you even thinking about it? Just do it the right way and move on.*

The same thing happens when I get into an argument with my wife. A voice in my head will say, "All right. This is it. I've had it. I'm tired of being the one who has to apologize. This time I'm taking a stand. If somebody needs to apologize, it's going to be her."

I'll stew that way for a few minutes. Then I'll finally come to my senses. *This is stupid. Neither of us is going anywhere. We're not giving up on this relationship. Now I'm just miserable. I'm getting nothing out of holding on to my anger. Just go apologize so you can work this thing out.*

It's amazing how often we struggle with what we *want* to do versus what we know we *ought* to do. I'm grateful that because of my father, I always have an example of which one to choose.

4

FAMILY COMES FIRST

*The most important thing in life
is knowing the most important things in life.*
DAVID F. JAKIELO

ONE OF MY DAD'S MANY TALENTS is the ability to see past relatively insignificant issues and get to the core of a problem. As a businessman, he believed in the 80/20 rule: 80 percent of a company's sales come from 20 percent of its customers. He applied it more broadly too, saying that too many people spend 80 percent of their time on 20 percent of their problems. His advice to colleagues at work and to us kids at home was the same: "You need to focus on the areas that are most productive."

I'm sure that approach was one of the reasons Dad was promoted in 1975 to president of the entire Bell & Howell company. The board of directors had learned what kind of businessman Dad was, and decided he was the guy to lead them to a brighter future.

I had just finished eighth grade in Arcadia. And when Dad

announced that we were going to give Kenilworth another try, I was all in. I knew it was a great opportunity for him. I was more mature than before and feeling great. Mom was doing better too. She even flew out and picked a house for us in our former neighborhood—if you took a path through our old backyard in Kenilworth you could get to the backyard of our new house. Bruz was starting his sophomore year at the University of Southern California, and Kristy was working and had moved to her own apartment, so they'd be staying in California. I knew I'd miss them, but I'd still have Mom, Brad, and Ray around. I hadn't had any depression issues since the last move, so I figured this time around I was good to go.

Illinois' New Trier East was a four-year high school, so I went out for freshman football full of optimism. We had a great team. We fell short in our first game because we lost track of downs as we were driving for what should have been the winning score, but we recovered from that setback to win every contest the rest of the season.

Since Bruz was a linebacker, I figured that was where I belonged, too. But I discovered it wasn't the right fit for me. I didn't have the speed for it. I also had the wrong mentality. A linebacker wants to avoid contact and shed blockers until he finds and tackles the guy with the ball. I had the habit of moving toward contact.

This difference reminds me of a play during my fourth season with the Oilers. We were hosting the Buffalo Bills in the Astrodome in our last game of the season. I was lined up against Bruce Smith, the Bills' Hall of Fame defensive end, and simply the best player I ever battled on the line. On this play, Smith beat me so fast that the rest of our linemen were still backing up into pass-protect mode when Bruce hit our quarterback, Warren Moon, and forced a fumble. I saw the ball on the ground and picked it up. I probably could have run for a first down, but I was so angry about getting beat that I wanted to inflict pain on somebody. I went right at the Bills' nose tackle, Fred Smerlas, and gave him an easy tackle. That pretty much summed up my approach on the field—I always wanted to hit somebody.

I played some linebacker for New Trier East during practices, but I'm not sure I ever did in a game. My main contribution instead was as an offensive tackle. Though I'd played a bit on the offensive line for the Kenilworth Rebels during our previous time in Illinois, this was my first significant exposure to it. I discovered that I enjoyed it. I liked that there was a plan, that I knew on every play what I was supposed to do. Instead of reacting, I was initiating. I also liked that success wasn't based just on raw talent, but that so much of it revolved around technique and fundamentals. I knew that the more I mastered those, the better I would be as a player. Offensive lineman wasn't the most glamorous position in football, but there was an order to it that appealed to me.

That freshman season was also when I picked up a skill that would become one of my defining contributions as a college and NFL player. One of the assistant coaches, a man we called "Coach K," was a short guy with a mustache and wire-rimmed glasses. Coach K had a crusty demeanor and was what you'd call old school. Only later did I find out that underneath, he was soft as a teddy bear. At the end of one of our first practices, he called out, "Who here can long snap? Who's interested in learning?"

I had never done long-snapping, which is the role of a center who hikes the ball about fifteen yards to the punter or seven to eight yards to the holder for a field goal or extra-point kick. But those lessons from my dad about volunteering had sunk in. I found myself saying, "Yeah, I'd like to try it."

It turned out I was a natural. Some guys have trouble with the snap, either bouncing the ball to the punter or snapping it over his head, but I was pretty consistent with putting it in the right spot. The idea is to get the ball there accurately and as fast as possible. It's a wrist shot, explosive and short, like a catcher throwing to second base. My baseball background could be the reason I caught on so quickly.

I wonder if I'd have been as eager to volunteer if I'd known what was to come. I became our team's long-snapper for the rest of my high school career. In college, I snapped for field goals my last three years and on punts in practices. Then in the NFL, while the rest of the guys on offense got a breather during kicks, I snapped and sprinted down-field on punt coverage for my first fifteen years and snapped on field goals for all nineteen years of my career. Those last few years, Kevin Long, my teammate on the Titans and fellow offensive lineman, was the punt team long-snapper. Kevin and I both ended our professional playing days the same year, 2001.

In today's NFL, long-snappers are specialists. Nobody plays both on offense and as a long-snapper. I guess you could say that Kevin and I were dinosaurs, the last of a dying breed. But I enjoyed long-snapping and took a lot of pride in it. It freed up another roster spot for someone who could contribute elsewhere. To me, long-snapping was just another way to help the team win.

•   •   •

Since moving back to Illinois, Dad was busier than ever as head of the company, but I found an unexpected way to bond with him that year. In the past, I'd always gone out for basketball once football season ended. As the time for the start of basketball practices approached, I thought back to my lack of enthusiasm for the sport from the year before. Dad remembered it too.

"Bruce, what are you going to do now?" he asked. "Are you going to play basketball?"

"I'm not sure," I said. "I'm not completely sold on that."

My dad got a gleam in his eye. "Why don't you wrestle?"

Dad, of course, was a three-time college conference champion in wrestling. He was unbeaten all four years he wrestled at Georgia Tech.

Just before we'd left Kenilworth when I was in seventh grade, I'd wrestled for a week in my physical education class. I did well and enjoyed it, though I was out of shape because I'd just gotten the cast off my leg after the football injury. But once we got back to Arcadia, I focused on other sports.

Now that we were in Kenilworth again, where wrestling was a big deal, I decided to give it a try. I went out for the freshman team. Since Dad had encouraged me, I figured I should take advantage of his expertise and ask for some tips. On our living-room floor, he showed me some of his moves. Most of us on that team were new to the sport and I quickly saw the fruits of Dad's instruction at practice. *Wow*, I thought. *This stuff really works.*

> *The first time I ever wrestled with Bruce as a kid, I knew he had the potential to play pro football if he wanted to. "This guy's going to be trouble someday," I said. And he was. But if you want me to try to explain our family's success in football, all I can say is I taught all my kids the same thing: Whatever you're doing, don't quit. Apply yourself. Be responsible. Show up and do it like you mean it. I expected a lot out of them and they lived up to it. I'm proud of every one of 'em.*
>
> CLAY MATTHEWS SR.

Those living-room lessons were a great way for the two of us to connect. No one else in our family had wrestled, so this was something that just Dad and I shared. I knew it meant a lot to me, but I didn't realize how much it meant to him until the weekend of my first matches.

On Friday night I defeated another freshman in my initial match in the 167-pound weight class. At the time I was five foot ten and about 165 pounds. Mom and Dad weren't able to be there, but they did come to the next one on Saturday afternoon.

We were at a dual meet that Saturday and the other team didn't have a freshman in the 167-pound weight class, so I'd already won by forfeit. Our sophomore team didn't have a 185-pound wrestler, so our opponent had already won his match by forfeit. The two coaches talked: "Hey, since these guys didn't get a chance to wrestle, why don't we let them square off in an exhibition?"

Our coach asked me about it. My opponent was a year older and twenty pounds heavier, but I didn't hesitate. "Sure," I said, "I'll do it." After my victory the night before, I was feeling pretty good about myself. After one match, I'd already developed some ego over my wrestling ability. I thought, *Hey, I'm 1–0. I'll take on all comers.*

Then I saw who I was up against. The guy was blond, huge, and ripped. He looked like Ivan Drago, Dolph Lundgren's character in *Rocky IV*. I was afraid he might take my head off.

My fears were well founded. Once the match started, this guy dominated me. Early in the second period, he was ahead of me 13–0. I didn't know many moves and was on my back most of the time, but I wasn't going to just give in and let the guy pin me. "Ivan" was frustrated because he couldn't finish me off.

He got so frustrated that midway through the second period, he lifted me off the mat and body-slammed me onto my shoulder. The referee blew his whistle, calling a time-out and awarding me my first point—a penalty against my opponent.

This was ugly. I couldn't help thinking, *What am I doing out here?*

My coach came over to talk to me during the time-out. "Hey Bruce, you all right?" he asked quietly.

"Yeah," I said, breathing hard. "I'm all right."

"Hey," he said, "if you say you can't go on, they'll end the match and you'll be awarded the win."

For a split second, I actually considered it. Then I shook my head. *No matter how good that sounds, you can't quit.*

The match continued. I didn't know it at the time, but my parents were dying in the bleachers. Mom was crying and Dad was thinking, *Oh no, what have I gotten him into?*

One of the great things about my foray into wrestling was my conversations with Dad. I told him about the pit in my stomach and the feeling of dread I had before every match, which always intensified, since I was always one of the last people to wrestle. I'd think, *Man, I want to be anywhere but here right now.* I would be nervous and anxious before football games too, even when I was forty years old, but nothing like what I experienced as a kid in wrestling.

Dad agreed with me. "The only thing worse than waiting to begin a wrestling match," he said, "is waiting to go into the ring to box. Those guys are trying to knock you out." I saw his point.

On the other hand, one of the greatest feelings in all of sports is that moment when you scrape and struggle to pin your opponent's shoulders against the mat and the referee slams his palm down with a *thwack* that echoes throughout the gym, signifying the end of the match. Suddenly, all the tension is released, replaced by an indescribable mix of exhilaration and relief.

I was expecting to be on the wrong end of that sound in my match against Ivan. It seemed just a matter of time. Then, no doubt because of his mounting frustration, my bigger and more talented opponent made a mistake. I was on all fours and he was on top of me, trying yet another maneuver to get me on my back. I felt his weight shift and realized he'd moved too high—that is, his center of gravity was too far forward. Without pausing to think about it, I reached back with my left arm, grabbed him somewhere, and flipped him. Suddenly, he was on his back and I was on top, squeezing his shoulders down as hard as I could.

Thwack!

The crowd let out a roar. I was in disbelief as the referee raised my arm, signifying that I'd won.

In the bleachers, Mom was smiling through her tears, while Dad had tears in his own eyes. He later told me he almost ran onto the mat to celebrate with me, something he would never do. When I greeted my parents a minute later, Dad said, "Bruce, that was one of the greatest things I've ever seen." Considering all that my dad had seen and done, it was quite a statement. The proud look on his face was one I'll never forget.

Only now, as a father, do I understand how emotional it must have been for my parents to watch their son getting whipped, and see him suddenly turn disaster into triumph. Nothing hurts more than seeing your children struggle, and nothing is more rewarding than seeing them succeed. Even today, I get choked up when I think about that day.

Dad and I continued our living-room lessons for the rest of the season. I'd come home from practice and we'd start messing around, Dad still wearing his suit pants, when he'd throw in a wrestling move I'd never seen before. "Dang," I'd say, "what is that?"

"That's an arm bar," he'd say. "It's a defensive move that can lead to a reversal. Here, I'll show you." And, pretty soon, I'd have another maneuver to add to my repertoire. Likewise, if I was having trouble with a certain opponent or move, he was able to demonstrate the perfect solution. He was my secret weapon.

I improved rapidly and finally began beating the teammate in my weight class. I finished the season with more wins than losses. But what I remember and cherish most from that season is the time I shared with my dad. It was when I began to truly understand how much he cared about me and our whole family. I'll take those memories over a victory on the mat every time.

● ● ●

Despite my athletic success, I struggled—again—with adjusting to life in Illinois. I remember being miserable during summer football practices and thinking, *I can't believe it. It's happening just like last time.* School was a grind once more. To my surprise, I was again depressed.

Mom seemed to be even worse off. Like before, she regularly withdrew to her room. After a few months, I reached a point where I felt like I'd turned a corner and might be able to stick it out. But that never happened for Mom. It wasn't that her depression had vanished when we were in California, but she was again having a much tougher time in Illinois.

Dad was fully occupied running Bell & Howell, yet he was also watching his family. He didn't like what he saw.

It must have been the spring of 1976 when Dad gathered us together and said, "I'm going to step down from Bell & Howell and figure something else out. We're going back to California." It couldn't have been an easy decision for him. He'd been named company president only a few months before. He was at the peak of his profession. But just as he did at the office, he acknowledged and identified the problem at home and was ready to show all of us where his priorities were. We moved back to Arcadia.

Dad says now that "it was no big deal," that he did it because "I loved my wife and family." But I know it was a big deal. I respect and admire him so much for making that choice. I appreciated it at the time, but as a husband and parent today I'm even more impressed. For so many men, our identities are wrapped up in our professions. They're how we tend to define ourselves. Dad had worked hard to achieve that top spot at Bell & Howell, yet he was willing to give it up so we would be in a better place physically and emotionally. With his actions, he was saying, "I'm willing to sacrifice and do whatever it takes to make sure my wife and children are taken care of, not just financially but emotionally. Family comes first."

In one sense, my father is a little like Coach K. You could call him crusty and old school. He carries himself like the tough guy that he is. But you know that on the inside, he has a soft spot for the people he loves.

Every day, I'm proud to call this man Dad.

5

SIBLING LESSONS

There can be no companion better than
a brother and no friend better than a sister.
AUTHOR UNKNOWN

MY DAD TAUGHT ME A LOT while I was growing up, as did my mom. But my parents weren't the only teachers in the Matthews household. In his or her own way, each of my siblings had a profound influence on my life.

Dad was my hero in the family, but Bruz was my role model, the guy I most wanted to be like. Bruz brought out my competitive spirit in our numerous battles against each other. But more than that, he showed me the dedication and discipline required to achieve success at the highest levels.

Since Bruz was the son of an NFL player and had such a great career, some people probably assumed that he was a natural or that his football accomplishments came easy. That simply wasn't so. Bruz was a late bloomer physically. He weighed 150 pounds in ninth grade and, at first glance, probably didn't lead anyone to believe that he was a future NFL star. But he more than made up for that with preparation and drive.

Long before year-round workouts became the rage, Bruz was doing them. He had a strict regimen. Nearly every day after school, he'd hop on his 125cc Suzuki motorcycle and ride to the Pasadena YMCA to lift weights. He ran sprints or distances most days at school too. The workouts paid dividends—he quickly got faster, bigger, and stronger. He was dedicated and willing to do whatever it took to be a great player. Since I was watching everything my brother did and wanted to imitate him, I began to understand what was required if I wanted to be great too.

When Bruz was a sophomore, he played middle linebacker for Arcadia's JV football team and was named MVP. He played for the varsity in his junior year, then came our first move to Illinois. I can't help wondering what ran through the New Trier East football coach's mind when my dad first introduced Bruz to him and the coach began to realize the gift he'd just been presented. I had a blast watching Bruz star at middle linebacker and running back his senior season. The team went undefeated, won the Suburban League title, and was named state champion. Even better from my perspective, Bruz was named a high school All-American.

My brother signed a letter of intent to go to Georgia Tech, Dad's alma mater, after forging a bond with defensive coordinator Maxie Baughan. But when Georgia Tech fired its coaching staff, Bruz reconsidered. Not long after, he got an invitation to visit the University of Southern California. The USC campus was only twenty-five minutes from our house in Arcadia, so it felt like home. Soon, Bruz was officially a Trojan.

Naturally, my brother had a great career at USC. He played regularly as a freshman while the team won the Rose Bowl and national title. At the end of his senior season, he was named a college football All-American. As always, I loved watching his games, this time at the mammoth Memorial Coliseum. The pros were watching too. In 1978 the Cleveland Browns made Clay Matthews the twelfth pick of the NFL draft.

On the one hand, it was hard to believe that the funny wise guy who liked to read comic books and talk smack with me was now a professional football player. But on the other hand, it seemed almost inevitable. Bruz had filled out at six foot two and 245 pounds when he joined the Browns. But the bigger factor was that once Bruz set a goal, he would not be denied the ability to reach it. He was just as dedicated as a student in high school and at USC, where he was an academic All-American in business administration. Today, he's still dedicated to being the best husband to Leslie, and father to Jennifer, Kyle, Brian, Clay III, and Casey, that he can be. His example drove me to be a better player and person.

I lived near Bruz in the Los Angeles area for the rest of my high school years, four years of college, and first eight years as a pro during the football off-season, which offered multiple benefits. It allowed us to continue our rivalry in every sport and activity we could imagine. That mutual and powerful will to win almost turned into disaster in the weeks after my brother's rookie year with the Browns. I've already mentioned that during the hundreds of basketball games we played against each other while growing up, I'd never beaten Bruz. Not even once. You can imagine how badly I wanted to end that streak.

We were playing another game of one-on-one at an elementary school. Bruz had finished his first year with the Browns and I was a high school senior. At this point, I was bigger than my brother at six feet five inches and 250 pounds. I used my height and weight to my advantage and was almost shocked to realize that I was winning the game, 8–3. Since we always played to ten, I needed only two more buckets to achieve a lifetime goal. *Oh, my gosh,* I thought, *I'm finally going to beat him.*

Then we both jumped for a rebound. I landed first. Bruz landed on my foot and slipped off. He began hollering and jumping around on one leg, obviously in pain. He'd rolled his ankle, one he'd already had problems with during the football season.

Horrible thoughts immediately ran through my mind. I was afraid I'd caused an injury that would force my brother to miss the next season—or worse, that the damage to his ankle might be permanent. *What have I done? I don't want to win that bad.* Bruz's wife, Leslie, was there too. I could see by the look on her face that she had the same awful fears.

It turned out my brother was more worried about his streak against me than his ankle. When the pain subsided after a few minutes, his first words were, "It was only 8–3, so that's not an official win." Once he said that, I knew he'd be all right.

For the record, I did defeat him in basketball soon after that day and have won the majority of our games since.

I loved the fact that, as I got older, I could still keep on competing against my brother. The greatest benefit to having Bruz live close by, however, was to my playing career. We worked out together some when I was in high school and college. Then, after I reached the NFL in 1983, we worked out together four days a week during the off-season. This was before most players trained year-round. Those sessions with Bruz were great. He pushed me to improve in running and endurance and I was able to push him to try to match me on the weights. When you're training with someone you aspire to be like, you don't let up. It gave me a mental edge going into each season. I was confident because I knew I'd done the hard work to get in shape. I also enjoyed relating to Bruz as a peer. He'd been my big brother for so long, and still was, but now I felt more like an equal.

A highlight of every NFL season was the two games we played against the Browns, and watching film of my brother before each contest. We'd phone each other on Wednesday or Thursday night of those weeks and talk about what we'd seen on film or whatever was on our minds. We weren't giving out tips—we both already knew about our mistakes. It was more about pointing out the good plays. I'd notice how smart he played and how much leverage he gained against his opponents. Bruz had an unorthodox but highly effective style. He had a way of dropping his hips to generate tremendous power. Meanwhile, he'd tell me, "You're too boring, man. It looks too easy for you, like you're not even trying." It was his way of complimenting me.

There's a lot of frustration that comes with being a professional athlete, especially when you're motivated to be the best. I could always talk about that with Bruce during those in-season calls, really about everything from performance to injuries to just letting off steam. If I had an issue, we wouldn't always find the answer, but Bruce always understood what I was going through. It was like having a built-in therapist you trusted.

CLAY MATTHEWS JR.

● ● ●

My brother was the best linebacker I ever played against, an All-Pro, a guy I believe deserves to be in the NFL Hall of Fame. But Bruz didn't become a great player by accident. It was his consistent commitment to developing his abilities over years of training that made him a star. He was determined to achieve excellence. I know that so much of the credit for any success I've achieved in football, as well as in life, has to go to him. I just tried to follow his example.

My other brothers, Brad and Raymond, were identical twins, with blond hair and green eyes. They were born two years before me. They were also both born with an intellectual disability. For my brothers, it essentially meant they didn't learn as easily or quickly as most people. As my dad has put it, they weren't handicapped, they just didn't have the same mental horsepower.

My parents said early on that Brad and Ray would be treated the same as the rest of us kids, which was one of their wisest decisions. The twins had the same chores and faced the same standards. They went to public schools with us, though they were enrolled in special-education classes.

As a kid, I was aware that Brad and Ray had extra challenges, but I didn't think a lot about it. They were part of the family, as athletic and competitive as any Matthews, so of course they joined in on our daily contests. Knee football, floor hockey, baseball in the backyard, basketball in the side yard—we played them all. The contests were two-on-two when Bruz was around. We played hoops nearly every night after dinner. The unofficial rule was no blood, no foul, so we beat on each other regularly and had our share of scraps. The twins didn't get as big as Bruz or me. Each was a little under six feet, with Ray heavier at about 205 pounds to Brad's 180. But they both could deliver a pounding as well as take one. When Bruz left for college and with Kristy already out of the house, they were my best buddies at home. Our favorite game in those years was Wiffle ball in the pool.

Though I had my struggles with adjusting to life in Kenilworth after our first move there, one thing that excited me was being teammates with Ray and Brad on the seventh-grade football team. They were primarily defensive linemen. Though neither played a lot, most of the guys on the team treated them well. My brothers enjoyed the camaraderie and the feeling of being equals with their teammates. They also enjoyed giving me a bad time after my injury that season. "Yeah, I'm sorry you broke your leg, Bruce," one or the other would say, "but I got to play after that." They were reminding me that even if I was no longer contributing to the team, they still were.

Another place my brothers excelled was in the Special Olympics. They each captured state Special Olympics swimming medals while in high school. They wanted to win as badly as Bruz and I did, battled just as hard during competitions, and celebrated just as much after a victory. Both got ejected from Special Olympics basketball and floor hockey games for fighting with opponents and arguing officials' calls. For better or worse, each was a Matthews to the core.

One of the things I admired about Brad and Ray is that they didn't sit around complaining about the disadvantage they'd been dealt. Brad was more personable and outgoing, but they both enjoyed whatever they were involved with. During my junior and senior years at Arcadia, they were the managers of the football team. It was fun to see my teammates joke with my brothers and give them a bad time—and to see Ray and Brad do the same with them. Their approach to life was a reminder to me to try to maintain a good attitude no matter what.

I've seen plenty of self-absorbed teenagers in my life, and I'm sure I often was one too. But having brothers with special needs helped show me that there would always be people around me who were less fortunate and who deserved my understanding, protection, and support. My experience with my brothers gave me a deeper sense of compassion.

That protective mindset came to the fore during an incident when I was still in Illinois as a ninth grader. I was at the high school and had just walked downstairs to a recreation area with Ping-Pong tables. I was shocked to see a stocky guy from my grade in Ray's face, making fun of him. Ray tried to walk away and this guy pursued him, still mouthing off and still in his face. I don't remember the guy's exact words, but they were demeaning comments about his disability.

Normally, I wasn't one to make a big scene or speech even if I disagreed with what someone was saying or doing. But this was just wrong—and it involved family. My attitude was, "Dude, I don't mind you teasing my brother or giving him crap. I give him crap all the time. But the second you start making fun of him, we're going to throw down."

Now my blood was boiling. I hurried over. "Hey, what are you doing, man?" I said. "He's my brother."

The bully turned away from Ray and toward me. He said something like, "You want a piece of me?"

We stared each other down for a few seconds. Frankly, part of me was scared and didn't want to be there. But the other part was furious and wanted to stand up for my brother. That's the side that won out. I popped the guy in the eye with a right. He dove at my legs, so I got on top of him and put him in a headlock. "You had enough?" I said. Before the guy could answer, someone intervened and pulled us apart. I know there are times when it's best to turn the other cheek, but this wasn't one of them. To this day, I can't stand watching people pick on someone who is disadvantaged.

Fortunately, moments like that were rare during our childhood. Most people treated Brad and Ray with kindness and respect, which always warmed my heart. They've each been a blessing to me in more ways than I can count.

●   ●   ●

If my sister, Kristy, had been on the scene when that guy was bullying Ray, she'd probably have given him a worse beating than I did. At five foot two, Kristy was the shortest of my siblings, as well as the fiercest. She was frank and willing to speak her mind. I learned early in life not to cross my sister.

Kristy was Matthews tough. When she was about twelve, she went horseback riding on a wet day, was thrown from the horse, and kicked in the head. The blow split open her brow line. I remember Kristy bleeding everywhere as Dad carried her into the house and got her ready for the trip to the hospital. All of us were worried, of course, except Kristy. She was more concerned about what all the blood would do to her leather jacket.

While I was growing up, my sister was someone I could talk to when I needed encouragement or advice. I remember discussing my shyness with girls. "Bruce, you're not a half-bad-looking guy," she'd say. "Just go up and talk to them like you're talking to me." I always appreciated it, but her encouragement seemed to go only so far. After one of our talks, I'd go to bed fired up and thinking, *I'm going to talk to that girl at school tomorrow*. Then I'd wake up with a pit in my stomach and think, *No way am I talking to that girl. I'm not even going near her*.

Another thing I learned from Kristy was that it was okay to stand up for myself, even for little things like asking for the right dinner at a restaurant if the waiter messed up the order. That was something I admired about her because it didn't come naturally to me. When we were kids, she was quick to defend Brad and Ray from any form of teasing and, after she got married and became a mom, she was just as quick to stand up for her kids, Devon and Ashley. Family definitely comes first for her. She's as loving as can be, but she also has an edge to her. That competitive family nature must have been passed down, because Ashley was an All-American soccer player for USC and team captain when the Trojans won the 2007 national title. She plays soccer professionally today.

I still talk regularly with Kristy and she still encourages me. I definitely value my relationship with her, as I do with all my siblings. They've been part of my life from the beginning. I'd do anything for them and know they'd do the same for me. It's true that no one gets to pick their family, but in my case I can't imagine choosing anyone else. I got the very best.

6

HUMBLED IN HIGH SCHOOL

In all the setbacks of your life as a believer,
God is plotting for your joy.
JOHN PIPER

IT WAS GREAT TO FINISH NINTH grade in California. New Trier East back in Illinois had an institutional feel. The buildings and hallways were walled in because of the harsh weather. But in Arcadia, everything was open. Our lockers and lunch space had a roof over them but were outside. At lunchtime, I could easily get in on an outdoor pickup basketball game on the nearby blacktop. Plus, New Trier East was a four-year high school, while Arcadia's was only three years. Instead of being a lowly freshman, I was suddenly one of the older, more experienced students at our junior high. I went from low man on the totem pole to feeling like a big shot.

I was big in another way: I was in the midst of a growth spurt. At the start of the school year I was five foot ten and 165 pounds, but by the end of the year I was six foot and two hundred pounds. My clothes didn't fit as well, but I didn't mind. I was getting leaner and adding strength.

Since I'd already been through the experience of starting high school in Illinois, I felt more confident as I looked ahead to entering high school the next year at Arcadia. Then I received news that made me even more eager to get started. The football coach invited me to practice with the varsity, while the baseball coach suggested I move up to the junior varsity team, where he said I had a great chance of starting at catcher. The baseball program at Arcadia was especially strong. *This is awesome*, I thought. *I'm back home where I'm comfortable and getting great opportunities in football and baseball.* Unlike in Illinois, I couldn't wait for school to start.

That spring and summer, I played Pony League baseball. Our team, King Meat (our sponsor was a butcher shop), was league champion for the second half of the season, so we faced off against the first-half winner in a single contest for the overall league title. The game was tied in the top of the final inning when I came up to the plate. The pitcher threw a fastball and I nailed it for a home run, which turned out to be the game winner. That ball traveled a long way. Urban legend has it flying over the left fielder's head, then over the playground beyond the outfield, and then over the elevated railroad tracks beyond that. If that were true we'd be talking Babe Ruth territory, maybe five or six hundred feet. No way did I hit it that far as a ninth grader—but I have to admit I haven't done much in the years since to dispel the rumor.

Finally, it was August and time for football. Arcadia's head coach and athletic director was Dick Salter, a no-nonsense type who would say when you went to get a drink of water, "Don't swallow any of that, just spit it out." The preseason included five days of two-a-day practices known as Hell Week. Each practice was an hour long and consisted of grass drills at six stations: pushups, bear crawls, burpees, up-downs, and more. At the end of each hour, everybody on the team ran eight "gassers," forty-yard sprints down the field and back, down a second time and back again. If even one player didn't finish within the determined time limit, the whole team had to run gassers again. That week was brutal.

I was always quiet on the field. I never talked back to my coaches. I'm sure they thought I had a great attitude. But there were times when that whistle blew and the coaches lined us up for another sprint that I thought, *What? Are you kidding me?* I'd ride my bike home exhausted after those practices and ask myself, *Why do I play football? I hate this.* But those of us who stayed with the program definitely developed a bond. I'm sure that had a lot to do with our shared "survival" experiences on Arcadia's football fields. Today I'm still close with several of my high school teammates, especially my buddy Dave Samarzich.

"Sam" was just fun to be around, a guy who would say and do things I never would. Before home games, we'd eat at my house, then go to my room and get fired up by listening to the soundtrack of the original *Rocky* movie. A few years later, Sam was on the football team at Pasadena City College. I told him I was coming to one of his games. Sam wasn't a starter, but because I was there, he inserted himself into the game by telling another player the coach wanted him out. Sam talked about the Arcadia Apaches so much in junior college that he became affectionately known as "Apache Sam."

In 1976, Sam was on Arcadia's freshman/sophomore football team, while I was thrilled and honored to make the varsity squad.

The only other sophomore on the varsity was a running back, Jim Mohr, so I was in rare company. I was on the defensive line in the first game and got in on probably ten or twelve plays. I thought I did all right. But on the Monday after the game, Coach Salter called me into his office. "Bruce," he said, "I know you're not going to like this, but we're going to send you down to the sophomore team. We want you to play every down. That's exactly what you need."

I couldn't believe what I was hearing. I was crushed. I was so proud of making that team. Now I felt as though my world had collapsed. I still remember walking out to that first practice with the sophomore team, seeing the surprised look on the faces of some of my friends, and feeling like a failure.

I was so angry during those last seven or eight games I played for Arcadia's sophomore team. I abused my opponents, taking out my frustrations by playing as hard as I could. Not surprisingly, the more I played, the more I developed my skills.

Wrestling season was a different and better story. I was still growing—after Christmas, I was up to 210 pounds—so I wrestled at heavyweight. My experience the year before in Illinois, combined with perfecting the techniques my dad taught me, allowed me to thrive. I won the Pacific League title that season, though I lost in the first round of the state playoffs. I went through the usual anxiety and stress before my matches, but overall I enjoyed it.

Another part of my enjoyment at that time was my anticipation of baseball season. I still harbored dreams of a career as a big-league catcher and the baseball coach's prediction that I might win a starting role with the JV team still rang in my ears. Maybe I had a chance to someday catch for the San Francisco Giants—why not?

What I didn't realize was that I was setting myself up for another major disappointment.

Part of the blame was due to my wrestling success. The California Interscholastic Federation wrestling tournament lasted a full two weeks beyond the regular season, causing me to miss all of Arcadia's baseball preseason. When I showed up for practice just before the games started, the coach pulled me aside. "Bruce," he said, "you've missed all this time and you're behind the other guys, so we're going to put you on the sophomore team."

Once again, I was crushed. If I felt like a failure before, now it seemed as though I couldn't do anything right.

My season soon went from bad to worse. I'd never experienced back trouble, but during my first practice I had a spasm. The abrupt transition from wrestling to baseball must have caused me to tweak something. I never saw a doctor about it, but it bothered me the rest of the season and contributed to my terrible start. I managed just one hit in my first twenty-five at-bats. Our team was pretty good, but I felt as if I wasn't contributing.

My junior season of football was much more satisfying. I picked up the nickname "Horse," and started on the varsity as an offensive and defensive tackle, as well as the team's long-snapper. The only time I came off the field was on kickoffs and kickoff returns. We did well in league play, then we went on to win three playoff games to advance to the CIF Coastal Section finals. We came up short in that title game, losing to Long Beach's Millikan High, 34–14. Even so, it was a great season overall.

In wrestling, I built on the momentum I'd established the year before. I went undefeated during the league season and expected to do really well at state. But to advance, I first had to defeat an opponent in the league title match that I'd beaten before. I didn't expect to have much trouble, but I got a little too full of myself. Heavyweights usually stay with the basics on the mat and don't do throws, which involves lifting an opponent and "throwing" him down on the mat. But I enjoyed employing those fancy moves and tried it. My opponent's arm slipped out. Instead of me throwing him, I landed on my back. He earned a two-point takedown and three-point near fall. I lost the match, 9–7.

My season was over, and though I didn't know it then, so was my wrestling career. Due to budget cuts, the school dropped the program after that season. We have a picture of me walking out of the gym after that match. I'm next to my dad, my head down. Even now, when I see that photo, it brings back all the disappointment of that day.

My junior year was also my last season in organized baseball. I was still upset over my experience the season before, so I didn't go out for the high school team. I did play that summer in my final year of Colt League eligibility and enjoyed it, but I'd figured out by then that football was my best sport. If there was any doubt, it was resolved my last game. I was part of a Colt All-Stars series against a team from Covina. In one game, I tried to score from third base on a ground out. The ball reached the catcher before I slid into home plate. I was clearly out, but what upset me was the catcher making what I thought was an unnecessarily hard tag as I was lying in the dirt.

In the final game of the All-Stars series, I again found myself on third base. When I took a big lead, the pitcher noticed and whipped the ball to the third baseman. I was caught in a rundown. *All right*, I thought. *I've had it. I'm six foot four and 235 pounds, so I'm going to use it.*

I sprinted for home. The throw went to the catcher, the same guy who'd tagged me hard before. There was no slide this time—I slammed into his chest, a clean hit, and sent him flying at least five feet. To his credit, he held on to the ball. Once again, I was out.

For the first time in my life, I heard jeers directed at me by the crowd. "Hey," one yelled, "this isn't football!"

"I guess this confirms it," I told myself. "I'm not a slippery, sliding base stealer. I'm a guy that likes contact and runs through people. Football truly is my future."

From that point on, my athletic focus was on football.

After our success the year before, expectations were high for Arcadia's football team going into my senior season. Then we lost our first three games and people were down on us. When a reporter interviewed me, the tone of her questions left me feeling personally accused, as if she were saying, "You're not playing at a high enough level." I kept my cool during the interview, but afterward I thought, *Man, that just ticks me off.* Once again I was feeling humbled by life.

I talked to my dad. "Well," he said, "what are you going to do about it? You've got a couple of options. You can let it get you down or you can come out swinging and give your best on the field every opportunity you get." I knew how he'd responded to challenges in his life. It helped inspire me to fight back and show anyone who was watching that we were better than what we'd demonstrated so far.

The whole team must have been fed up with losing, because we won the rest of our league games and again swept through the play-offs to reach the CIF Coastal Section finals. Our opponent in the title game was Compton, a school we'd squeaked by in a playoff game the season before, 6–3. Our defense was great in that championship contest, but I had a couple of plays I wish I could take back. The first was in the first half. I was blocking for a punt return and when I looked up, the ball was coming down, right to me. Returning a punt is a lineman's dream. I was about to catch it and planned to take it to the house. Instead, someone bumped me just before the ball arrived. The ball bounced off my shoulder and Compton recovered the fumble.

The game was tied 7–7 in the third quarter, when we were stopped on our twenty-yard line and had to punt. That's when I made my second big mistake. Maybe I was too hyped up. Whatever the reason, for the only time up to that moment, or in all the years since, I snapped the ball over our punter's head. Kerry Burns corralled the ball in our end zone, tried to run it out, and got tackled on the one-yard line. Compton scored a touchdown seconds later to take the lead. We did tie the score at fourteen, and it was still tied at the end of regulation, but they scored a touchdown in overtime. When we couldn't do the same on our possession, Compton took the championship.

That bad snap stuck with me for a long time, as did so many of the setbacks I endured in high school. I was hurt and angry over failing to stay on the varsity football team, and not even getting a chance at joining the JV baseball team. I was disappointed with the way my wrestling career ended and with my errors in my final high school football game, especially when we came so close to winning.

With the help of my dad's advice, I did learn to use my shortcomings and mistakes as motivation to do better. I was able to channel some of my anger and frustration into improving my performance. But each of those disappointments stung for a long time. It was a humbling period.

If I'd spent a little more time looking around and thinking about what my family was going through, I might have realized that for each of us, the journey through life is often humbling. After all, my dad had just given up his job as company president. He continued to commute between Illinois and California for the rest of that school year, before taking a new position as an executive at Aerojet General. My mom improved again after we moved to California, but she still had her struggles with depression. Brad and Ray were fighting the challenges that come with intellectual disabilities. My disappointments and frustrations didn't compare to theirs.

I've since learned that when our pride or ego starts inflating, life has a way of reminding us that we're not in charge and things do not always go our way. Those harder times may be filled with setbacks and roadblocks, but the process of overcoming and clearing them builds our character and makes us more effective at whatever we're trying to achieve.

When I was sent down to the sophomore football team, I developed much more quickly as a lineman because I had the opportunity to play every down. I was so disappointed then, but I see now that it was the best thing for me. Likewise, my difficulties in baseball began to sour me on the idea of becoming a big leaguer and helped point me in the direction of football, the sport I was ultimately best suited for. My defeat in my last wrestling match and even in my final high school football game were reminders that I shouldn't get too cocky or ever think that I have everything under control. Those were tough lessons, but I benefited from each one.

Despite my athletic setbacks and shyness with girls, I enjoyed high school overall. I had a lot of fun hanging out with Sam and another friend, Dan Nickovich. Going into my senior year, though, I realized I needed to start looking to the future. I figured I had a chance to play college football somewhere. During that final season, I began thinking I might even get a scholarship to play. Though Bruz was in his rookie year with the Browns at the time, the NFL wasn't at all on my radar. I did not see myself in that class.

Though it was nothing like the recruiting process that kids go through today, I did start receiving letters of interest from West Coast colleges in the summer before my senior year. After football season, I was named to the All-Pacific League and All-CIF teams. In January I made official visits to Arizona State, California, and UCLA. It looked like I might become a Cal Bear, but I still held hope of hearing from one more school—the University of Southern California.

In those days USC was a national powerhouse. The Trojans, led by legendary coach John Robinson, had been voted the nation's top team the season before by United Press International. They were so well regarded that they could swoop in late in the recruiting process and pick up almost whomever they wanted for their program. That's what I hoped would happen to me.

I'd received a letter from USC back in November, but no offer. Then Coach Robinson came to our home for a visit in January. He was one of those people who, when he spoke, you sat up and listened. I already had great respect for Coach Robinson after meeting him at Bruz's senior-year banquet. He was obviously a highly successful coach. He told stories that were funny and entertaining but also had a life message. I still held Coach Robinson in high regard more than two decades later when I sat next to him at an NFL Hall of Fame event. I was forty years old but felt as nervous and in awe of him as when I was eighteen. When he asked me to call him John, I said, "Coach, I can't call you John. You're always going to be Coach to me."

After Coach Robinson's visit to our home, it was obvious that the USC football staff was at least interested in me. I wondered if they were recruiting me mostly because I was the brother of Clay Matthews. I wanted to go there, but I was also afraid of not being able to meet USC standards. If I did get an offer, I hoped I could make the travel team or maybe get into some games for mop-up duty. My dad seemed to be aiming higher. "Do you want to play with the best?" he said. "Do you want to find out where you really stand with this thing? Then go to USC."

I was invited to the USC campus for a visit in late January and, when they offered me a scholarship while I was there, I accepted on the spot. I'd been humbled more than once during my high school years. I knew I wasn't at the top of the USC coaches' list. None of that mattered. I was pumped up. I would follow in my brother's footsteps by wearing the cardinal and gold and watching Traveler, the USC mascot, gallop around the Coliseum after every touchdown.

I was officially a Trojan.

7

A BOY AMONG MEN

Masculinity is not something given to you, but something you gain. And you gain it by winning small battles with honor.
Norman Mailer

The summer after my high school graduation, I played in the Rose Bowl in California's high school Shrine All-Star game. Our team won 35–15 with the help of a pretty decent quarterback named John Elway.

If I thought I was in good company in that game, I was star-struck when I started practicing with the regulars at USC. I'd actually scouted them several times during their spring practices on the USC campus. I tried to blend into the crowd as I watched. I realized right away that the linemen were bigger, stronger, and way ahead of me in terms of technique—not surprising, considering their success the year before.

USC's starting offensive line in 1979 would be Anthony Munoz and Keith Van Horne at tackle, Brad Budde and Roy Foster at guard, and Chris Foote at center. Munoz, six foot seven and 280 pounds, would be taken third overall in the NFL draft that followed the season. Budde would win the Rotary Lombardi Award as the nation's outstanding college lineman or linebacker and be drafted eleventh overall. Van Horne and Foster were also eventual first-round picks. All five would be highly successful professionals. As a high school kid watching these massive dudes demonstrate their skills on the practice-field grass that spring, you could say I was a bit intimidated.

Four months later, I stood on that same grass myself. I felt I had a lot to prove. I'd read accounts of the USC recruiting class and noticed I was always far down on the list of heralded prospects. I figured many of my new teammates knew me only as Clay Matthews' little brother.

The freshmen started training in August a few days before the rest of the team. We were put through conditioning tests that began with a forty-yard dash. My time was six seconds flat. To put that in perspective, all the elite guys were finishing under five seconds, some well under that. Clearly, I would not be among the team's swiftest members. They had us run the forty a second time, and I again recorded a time of exactly six seconds. At least I was consistent.

Those tests were followed by eight gassers—more forty-yard sprints with a half-minute rest between each one. I huffed and chugged my way through them, slowing down more each time. I knew I was impressing no one. *Oh, my gosh,* I thought, *the coaches are probably saying, "What have we done by taking this kid?"*

I turned eighteen during preseason training. Munoz and Budde were already married—I felt like a boy among grown men. I was not prepared for the intensity of the practices. I knew college ball would be a step up for me, but the dedication and professionalism these guys displayed quickly got my attention. I realized I had to meet the standard or I'd be left behind.

I didn't help my cause on the day before our first game. We were in Lubbock to play Texas Tech. I was excited to have made the travel squad since the National Collegiate Athletic Association limited how many players could go to away games. Unfortunately, I developed an earache just before we were scheduled to leave for practice at the stadium. I lay down for what I thought would be a minute on my hotel bed. When I awoke, my roommate and the team bus were gone. Panicked, I caught a ride from someone and hurried down the ramp to the locker room as players began to emerge. I thought I'd made it unnoticed until I ran into Hudson Houck, our offensive line coach. I Ie chewed me out good. There was nothing I could say.

A week later, I was messing around in the training room, lost track of the time, and was late for an offensive line meeting. Once again, Hudson Houck let me know my behavior was unacceptable. Getting on the wrong side of my position coach was the last thing I wanted to do. *Man,* I thought, *I am blowing this thing.*

Our team was so good that year that I did get to play often, usually in the fourth quarter because we were so far ahead. Going into our last conference game, we were undefeated. The lone blemish was a 21–21 tie against Stanford. Anthony Munoz suffered a knee injury in our first game and was replaced by freshman Don Mosebar, another future first-round NFL draft choice. Then Don had a knee injury of his own in practice on the Tuesday before our finale against UCLA. When Coach Houck informed me I'd be starting that Saturday, I was both thrilled and scared.

Wow. UCLA at the Coliseum. I've grown up watching my brother's games there. I'm just a kid. I don't belong out there.

I was keyed up when I called my dad that night. I expected him to be surprised and excited about me starting. Instead, he talked like he expected it. "You're going to do great," he said. "I know it." His matter-of-fact words calmed me down and gave me confidence that I was ready for the responsibility.

I played well enough against UCLA and we won, 49–14. It meant we'd square off against top-ranked Ohio State in the Rose Bowl on New Year's Day. Before the game, I noticed one of my heroes, USC alumnus and NFL Hall-of-Famer O. J. Simpson, at midfield. I walked over and introduced myself. I was thrilled to meet him. O. J. was very friendly and in the years since always chatted with me when we ran into each other. I've been shocked by all his issues over the last couple of decades.

Anthony Munoz, one of the classiest guys I've ever met, had rehabbed during the season and was healthy enough to start the Rose Bowl. I spelled him for a couple series and was on the field for our first touchdown, a fifty-three-yard pass from Paul McDonald to Kevin Williams in the second quarter. Yet we trailed 16–10 in the game's final minutes. That's when all those studs on our offensive line and running back Charles White, the Heisman Trophy winner that year, went to work. I had one of the best views in the stadium as my teammates marched down the field on one rushing play after another. From a yard out with less than a minute left, Charles leaped over everyone to score the winning touchdown. It was quite a finish to my first season of college football.

●　　●　　●

Between my conversations with Coach Houck over my tardiness and the fiasco over being caught cheating on that physics test, you could say my first college semester was less than perfect. But I began getting my act together during second semester, both on the field and off. I thought about switching from industrial engineering to an easier college major, but decided to stay with engineering. Though I could have been a stronger student and didn't fully apply myself until my senior year, I did start doing a better job in class.

I also stepped up my effort in football. Munoz, Budde, and Foote were all graduating, so there were openings on the offensive line. Those spring practices were tough—full contact and balls out. But even though I was tired, sore, and beat up, I told myself, "You can work through this. You've got to keep bringing it." The hard work paid off. I won a starting guard spot for the fall.

Going into my sophomore year, it felt like I had momentum, that most of my life was moving in a positive direction. The lone exception was in the romance department. I think I'd asked two girls out in my life, both at the end of my senior year of high school, and neither one had said yes. I remained shy as ever around the girls and mostly hung out with my football buddies. I was like a race car that kept stalling at the starting line.

There *was* a girl I'd noticed freshman year who ate in the same campus dining hall as I did. She was blonde, very pretty, and always seemed to be joking with her friends. She looked like she'd be fun to get to know. But to walk up and actually talk to her? I was not ready for that.

Then, during spring semester of my freshman year, I was walking through a parking lot near my dorm. A car came around the corner and the driver braked to avoid hitting me. I looked to see who had almost hit me—it was the same girl I'd noticed before. She waved.

I looked behind me—no one there.

Oh gosh, is she waving at me?

That made me nervous, so I got out of there as fast as I could. Only later did I learn what the girl—Carrie Kitchen—thought as I hurried away, hands in my pockets: *Geez, you could at least wave back since I'm just trying not to run you over. What a jerk. Fine, Mr. Big-Time Football Player, don't wave at me. I don't care.*

Fast-forward to the night before classes began in September of my sophomore year. My memory is that I was walking down USC's "Fraternity Row" on Sunday with my teammate Kevin Roddy. Suddenly, two attractive girls came up and began talking with us. One was the blonde girl from the parking lot. I learned her name was Carrie. I'll call the other girl "Lisa." To my surprise, the girls stayed for a while and kept chatting. *This is pretty cool,* I thought. *I wonder why they're hanging out with us.* Later, one of my buddies asked me about them: "What do you think? Are you interested?"

"Sure," I said. "They're both great!"

My wife tells a slightly different version of the story. Her memory is that a few days before that Sunday night, one of my buddies told Lisa that I wanted to go out with her. Carrie, being a good friend, joined Lisa on a search for me that Sunday to try to get us together. Maybe I've got it wrong and my wife is right—it wouldn't be the first time. Or maybe someone asked one of my friends before that Sunday if I was interested in Lisa and he decided to answer for me—that wouldn't surprise me either.

Whatever the case, on the next Saturday night, Carrie and Lisa parked themselves near the front of a crowded campus pizza hangout after our home victory over South Carolina. They were looking for me so Carrie could again try to get me to bond with Lisa. What they didn't know, however, is that I was already there, sitting in a booth in the back. At one point the crowd parted and I spotted the two of them. "Hey," I said to teammate Rob Hedquist while pointing to Carrie—my courage might have been fortified by a bit of alcohol at this point—"Go ask that girl to come sit over here."

Rob did just that. He knew Carrie, and though it took a bit of convincing, he got Carrie to come to our booth filled with football players. She didn't know who had asked for her until a couple of players got up so she could sit next to me. *Holy smokes,* she thought. *Is Bruce the one I'm supposed to meet?*

When I saw Carrie, I started getting nervous again, just like in the parking lot. But before either of us had time to back out, Carrie had been escorted to her seat and we were both wedged in by my friends. Ready or not, we had to start talking.

At one point, Lisa came to the back and saw what was happening. Carrie felt terrible and tried to get my buddies to make room for Lisa too. "No, that's okay," Lisa said. "I'm going to get going." Meanwhile, my friends stayed right where they were. Carrie and I talked until closing that night. Then I walked her home.

I really enjoyed talking with Carrie. I was hooked. I got a friend to ask Carrie if she'd say yes if I asked her out—I guess having a third party involved made it seem like I'd feel less rejected if she said no. Fortunately, the word that came back was positive (Lisa convinced Carrie to accept the date). I'll let Carrie tell the next part of the story.

It was all arranged. When Bruce called and asked me out, I knew what he was going to say. I agreed to a first date at ten that Saturday night after he flew back from a game against the University of Minnesota.

On Saturday, I'm in my room. I'm waiting and waiting and the clock keeps ticking and ticking. No Bruce. It's finally getting close to midnight. Fine, *I think.* Go ahead and stand me up. Maybe you are a jerk after all. *I change into my sweats.*

The phone rings. It's Bruce: "Hi, what are you doing?"

"Well, I was thinking of going to bed soon."

"No, no, I'm coming to get you. We have a date."

"Our date was two hours ago."

Bruce explains that the flight was delayed and he's just gotten back.

"It's too late now."

"No, no, we can go to a midnight show." Bruce talks me into going. I get dressed again, he picks me up, and we see the only movie playing in Westwood, The Life of Brian. *After the movie, we're walking toward his car and I'm chatting away.*

Suddenly, with lightning reflexes, Bruce spins and grabs me with both hands, his grip firm. I freeze. "What are you doing?"

"Look down," he says.

I look. There's a taut wire stretched across the sidewalk in front of me at ankle height. It's apparently meant to block the entrance to a parking lot. If I had taken another step I would have done a faceplant into the asphalt.

Since Bruce saved me from harm as well as humiliation, I decide he isn't a jerk at all. He's actually a pretty nice guy. In fact, he's my hero.

Carrie and I started dating regularly after that. I called my mom to tell her about it. "Mom, I've met this girl," I said. "She's awesome." I soon realized that as far as I was concerned, this was it. I could see myself spending the rest of my life with Carrie. On my next visit home, I sat down with Mom. "This girl's really special," I said. "Mom, I've found her. She's the one."

Carrie and I were talking on the phone after a couple of months of dating and I found myself saying, "Yeah, I wouldn't mind marrying you."

"Really?" Carrie said in a surprised voice.

"Heck, yeah." From that point on, we talked often about marriage. You could say that my social life had taken a dramatic turn for the better.

In early December, Carrie came to Arcadia to meet my parents for the first time. It meant a lot to me that they loved her from the start. Mom started calling her "Sweet Carrie"—they hit it off right away. Dad showed his approval by displaying his unique brand of humor. He spun Carrie around and said, "You look like good breeding stock." I was relieved that Carrie wasn't offended and took it as intended. It was one more sign that she was the perfect girl for me.

● ● ●

My sophomore football season included several highlights as well. We started the year ranked fifth nationally and moved up as high as number two before a couple of late-season losses. I played well at times, but never felt entirely comfortable as a starter. I was still learning what was required to excel at the college level. Then, in our final game against second-ranked Notre Dame, I finally put it all together and played my best game of the season. Our running backs gained more than two hundred yards rushing and we beat the Fighting Irish, 20–3.

I was disappointed to see the season end. I'd come a long way. I was playing with more consistency and getting a handle on the fundamentals. I was beginning to believe I might actually become pretty good at this football thing.

My junior year was a lot of fun. I'd been in a studio apartment with Don Mosebar my sophomore year. Don and I moved into a bigger apartment with another roommate, Doug Branscombe. Doug was an industrial engineering major from New Hampshire and just as competitive as any of the guys on the football team. We played a lot of video games and tennis—whatever the competition, he hated to lose. He remains a good friend today.

That year was fun on the field as well. We had a tremendous rushing attack led by Marcus Allen, who became the first college running back to rush for over two thousand yards in a season. Blocking for Marcus was a pleasure. He was one of the toughest dudes around and one of the greatest I ever played with.

Marcus didn't talk much on the field. He just ran the ball hard, got up, walked back to the huddle, and did it again. He wanted to be the best at everything—not just running the ball, but blocking and even passing on trick plays. When we were in the NFL, I loved watching him take on a safety or linebacker on a blitz. He wasn't content to just block them. He tried to drop them. Playing with Marcus was one of the highlights of my football career.

Another teammate not nearly as famous, but just as dedicated, was Dave Holden. Dave was a walk-on, one of my best friends at USC and still a good buddy now. Like me, he loved the game, knew a lot about football history, and noticed the little things when we watched teams on film. I always had so much respect for the walk-ons. They rarely played, yet worked just as hard as the regulars.

That 1981 team came together quickly. In our third game, we were ranked first nationally and our opponent, Oklahoma, was number two. The teams battled back and forth, with Marcus gaining 208 rushing yards. It came down to the game's final play, when our quarterback, John Mazur, tossed a seven-yard touchdown pass to my freshman-year roommate, Fred Cornwell. We beat the Sooners, 28–24.

We stumbled a couple of times that season, losing to Arizona and Washington, before coming back for a 22–21 victory over UCLA. We took on Penn State in the Fiesta Bowl, including a couple of Nittany Lions who would be important in my future: Mike Munchak and Chet Parlavecchio. I'd never heard the kind of trash talk those guys dished out. They tackled Marcus for a loss on the first play and someone started yelling, "It's not your day, Marc! It's not your day!" No one ever called Marcus Allen "Marc." But I had to give them credit. They backed up the talk with a great game and beat us, 26–10.

Marcus deservedly won the Heisman Trophy that year. It was a thrill to be invited along with Don Mosebar, Roy Foster, and fullback Todd Spencer to New York's Downtown Athletic Club for the ceremony. I got to meet several previous Heisman winners. The whole weekend was awesome.

Roy was a senior that season and was chosen in the first round of the NFL draft by the Dolphins. When that happened, I thought, *Yeah, I can do this.* I'd played with Roy for three years and saw us as being in a similar class. For the first time, the idea of a career in the NFL started feeling less like a pipe dream and more like a reality.

● ● ●

I was a senior in fall 1982. Suddenly my college experience was flying by. I was so focused on doing well on the field and in the classroom that year that I didn't always appreciate what a special time it was. I wish now that I'd slowed down once in a while to savor it all.

The Trojans were ranked eleventh going into the season. I was named a preseason All-American and one of three team captains. We opened with a tough loss at Florida, 17–9. I had a great game with the exception of three penalties.

Our home opener was the next week against Indiana. In the second quarter, our quarterback, Sean Salisbury, was scrambling near the Indiana bench when their safety took him down with an especially hard hit. What was worse in my eyes, however, was when the safety stood over Salisbury, pointing down at him and celebrating the hit. I was trailing the play and saw it all. I was livid. Before I stopped to think about it, I ran full speed at the safety and just drilled him. Unfortunately, he was two yards out of bounds at the time.

A referee threw me out of the game. Then Lee Corso, now an analyst for ESPN's College GameDay but then Indiana's coach, got in my face and started yelling at me. I yelled back. It wasn't one of my proudest moments. After I calmed down, I was embarrassed. Carrie was at the game. So was my family. I felt I'd let my team down. Coach Robinson had to sit me down the next week and ask me to tone my passion down a notch. I felt terrible about it.

What's funny is that a few months later at one of the NFL combines, an official for one of the teams came up to me and said, "Hey man. You made yourself a lot of money by drilling that guy on the sidelines."

"What?" I said.

"The Indiana game. We liked that." Apparently my passion and willingness to stand up for a teammate got the NFL's attention. It just shows that there's a silver lining to every disaster.

Our record improved to 3–1 after wins over Oklahoma and Oregon. Then we beat Stanford at their place, 41–21, on October 16. The game was not my biggest highlight that weekend in the Bay Area, however.

I'd gotten permission from the coaches to stay an extra night so I could take Carrie to Ghirardelli Square by Fisherman's Wharf, where we had dinner reservations. I had a ring with me. I'd already asked Carrie's parents, Dr. Clyde Kitchen and his wife, Janet, if I could marry their daughter, and I'd received their blessing. My plan was to propose to Carrie during dinner, but even though I was sure I knew what she'd say, I was still nervous and just wanted to have it done. We were waiting near the restaurant on a park bench with a view of San Francisco Bay. I decided the time was now.

I pulled out the ring and got down on one knee.

"What are you doing?" Carrie said.

"Carrie," I said, "I've thought about this and I know I want to spend the rest of my life with you. You would make me the happiest man on earth if you would marry me."

She said yes.

I must have been a little distracted during our candlelight dinner. When we were finished and I got up to leave, our dishes started crashing to the floor. I'd accidentally tucked the tablecloth into my pants and was pulling it away when I stood. It was a great weekend anyway.

We finished the football season with a record of 8–3, including a 17–13 victory over Notre Dame at the Coliseum in my final game. I'm definitely proud of the fact that during my four years at USC I never lost to the Irish. When people ask me which opponent I most wanted to beat in college or the NFL, I usually say, "Whoever we were playing that week." But I have to admit that Notre Dame was near the top of my list of teams I wanted to see go down.

Another favorite memory of that last season is traveling to New York to tape the *Bob Hope Christmas Special* at Rockefeller Center. Every year, the show's producers flew in the Associated Press All-America team. We introduced ourselves one at a time on camera and had a moment with Bob. When my turn came, Bob said, "I understand you come from a football family." My scripted reply was, "That's right, Bob. My dad played for the 49ers and my brother plays for the Browns." Then I jogged off the stage.

My last semester of college was a whirlwind. There was a Pro Day at USC and NFL scouting combines, where pro teams had a chance to evaluate me and other prospective players. During a Pro Day before my senior year, I'd run a forty-yard dash in five seconds flat, shaving a full second from my time when I started at USC. I was pleased about that.

One of the combines was in Tampa, Florida. I was getting dressed when a man came up to me. "Hey Bruce, I want to introduce myself," he said. "I'm Bill Parcells, the new head coach of the New York Giants." This was of course before he'd led the Giants to two

Super Bowl championships and the Patriots to another Super Bowl appearance. I didn't know who he was.

"I just want you to know," he said, "that if you're still available we're going to take you with the number-ten pick in the draft."

That blew me away. By this time I figured I'd be drafted, but I had no idea teams were considering me at that level. The draft itself took place in New York on April 26. John Elway went first and Eric Dickerson second. The Giants never got the chance to follow through on Bill Parcells' words. The Houston Oilers chose me with pick number nine.

I didn't have a lot of time to think about what life might be like in Houston and the NFL. On May 13, I graduated from USC with my degree in industrial engineering. Two weeks and a day later, I was in a church in Carrie's hometown of Fullerton, California, sweating in a tuxedo and saying "I do" at the appropriate moment. Carrie had told the pastor who married us that she wanted a traditional ceremony, no jokes or shenanigans. The pastor kept his promise to do that—until the moment we were officially married. We were still walking down the aisle when we heard the organist, as the pastor had arranged, switch from playing the wedding march to the USC fight song.

I couldn't believe how much my life had changed in four years. I'd started college as a kid who lacked confidence in his football ability, was afraid to talk to girls, and was trying to figure out his place in life. Now I had a college degree, was about to join the NFL, and was married.

I was blessed beyond belief. I also had no idea how many more blessings—and heartaches—were just around the corner.

8

HEART AND SOUL

A mother is a person who seeing there are only four pieces of pie
for five people, promptly announces she never did care for pie.

TENNEVA JORDAN

THE HOUSTON OILERS, LED BY COLORFUL coach Bum
Phillips, unstoppable running back Earl Campbell, and defensive
stars Elvin Bethea, Gregg Bingham, and Robert "Dr. Doom" Brazile,
had an outstanding team at the end of the seventies. They twice came
within a single victory of the Super Bowl, losing in the playoffs in
both the 1978 and 1979 seasons to the eventual champion Pittsburgh
Steelers. Houston's fans rallied around their Oilers in an era dubbed
"Luv Ya Blue" by Campbell.

By 1983, however, the Oilers hardly resembled a perennial championship contender. They still had Campbell, but the coach was now
Ed Biles. The window of opportunity for those great Houston teams
had passed. The current Oilers squad was young and facing a period of
growing pains. I was supposed to be part of the new youth movement.

For the first couple weeks of training camp, however, I wasn't part of anything. The last thing I wanted was to get my career started on a bad note, but I did want to be paid a fair salary. Most professional football players make a pile of money, especially these days, but they also risk permanent injury every time they walk onto the field and never know when their career is going to end. My agent, Howard Slusher, and I agreed that the Oilers should have offered me a salary that fell between what the eighth and tenth picks in that year's draft received. In an era before the current wage-scale system for draft picks, the Oilers offered less.

Howard was known for clients who held out for better contracts and he advised me to do the same. He said I'd regret it if I didn't stand up for what was fair. I agreed and Houston's training camp started without me. I believed it was the right thing to do, but it was hard. I felt an obligation to be there, but I also didn't want to be taken advantage of.

Fortunately, the Oilers soon agreed to what we proposed, and I signed a four-year contract on July 25. I was twelve days late when I arrived in the middle of the night at the Oilers' camp at Angelo State University in San Angelo, Texas. I wondered what kind of reception I'd get from my new teammates at my first practice. For the most part, they ignored me. I think they were just trying to get through another day of Texas heat.

Our quarterback was veteran Archie Manning, a two-time Pro Bowler who's now just as famous for being the father of Peyton and Eli Manning. I hardly expected Archie to even know who I was, so I was shocked when he came over at the end of that first practice and said, "Hey Bruce, why don't I take you out for a beer and pizza?"

As a kid, I'd watched Archie Manning during his college days at Ole Miss and then in the pros for the New Orleans Saints. I couldn't believe that just the two of us were sitting down for pizza. It was a wonderful gesture that helped an uptight rookie begin to feel like part of the team.

More of the Oilers made me feel welcome as the preseason went on. We all stayed in the campus dorms and someone had stocked a refrigerator with beer. Each night, fifteen or twenty guys gathered around the fridge to just talk and get to know each other. It was surreal for me to be sitting with guys I'd watched play on television. Those sessions created an important spirit of camaraderie, not just for me but for the whole team.

I needed all the team spirit I could get that preseason. Other than my broken leg back in seventh grade in Illinois, I'd never suffered an injury in football, but in the fourth quarter of our first preseason game, veteran left tackle Doug France threw a defender my direction. The player hit me in the back of my right leg. Suddenly, I felt shooting pain in my ankle and knee. I was sure it was serious. I was afraid I'd ended my NFL career before it had even started.

I missed the next two preseason games. Fortunately, my knee quickly got better. My ankle improved as well, though it bothered me some the rest of the year. With the help of a cortisone shot, I was able to play in our final preseason contest, a nationally televised affair against the Dallas Cowboys. I went into the lineup in the second quarter.

In those days, teams played their starters most of the way in the final preseason game to tune up for the regular season. Everyone went all out. Soon after I came in, acting on instinct, I made a cut block on a Dallas defender on a screen play. A cut block is when you dive for an opponent's legs to take him out of the play. It's an aggressive move that does include some risk of injury for the defender, but it's within the rules. (If you do the same to a defender who's already been engaged by another blocker, it's a chop block, which is against the rules.)

The player I cut turned out to be Ed "Too Tall" Jones. Too Tall was a handful at defensive end—six foot nine, 270 pounds, and a veteran All-Pro. After the play, I was walking back to the huddle when someone blasted me in the back and sent me sprawling. The culprit was Too Tall. "Hey rookie, don't you ever cut me!" he yelled while standing over me. "I just embarrassed you in front of the whole nation. You don't cut me!"

Oh man, I thought. *What is this all about?* I played against Too Tall a few more times before he retired, but he'd made his point. I never did cut block him again.

We opened the 1983 season against the Green Bay Packers, who'd won their division the year before. Since I'd missed most of the preseason, I was on the bench and John Schuhmacher started the game at right guard. "Shoe" was five years older than me. Ironically, he also went to Arcadia High School and played with my brother at USC.

Unfortunately for Shoe, during one play in the first half against the Packers, a pile of bodies fell on him. His leg was broken. I replaced him and started the next game—and, except for one season, I started every game after that for the next nineteen years. Shoe likes to say that "You never know what would have happened if I hadn't gotten injured in that Green Bay game. The streak might never have happened. Bruce might have been a first-round bust." Shoe is a great dude and we're still friends today.

That Packers game was a thrill. Not only was it my first NFL game, but both teams' offenses marched up and down the field. We nearly pulled off the upset, scoring three touchdowns in the final quarter to tie the game before losing on a field goal in overtime, 41–38.

Even though we'd lost, I almost felt like we'd won. Our young team had showed a lot of promise. I felt we might surprise some people. Our offensive line—Mike Munchak and me at guard, Harvey Salem and Doug France at tackle, and David Carter at center, along with Schuhmacher—didn't allow a quarterback sack for the game. Archie Manning took us all out to a steak dinner that week and said he'd do it every week we kept those defenders off him and recorded zero sacks.

It never happened again that season.

Our second game was against the Los Angeles Raiders in my old college home, Memorial Coliseum. That Raiders team was loaded—Jim Plunkett at quarterback, defensive stars such as Howie Long, Lyle Alzado, Mike Haynes, and Lester Hayes, and my former USC teammates Marcus Allen and Don Mosebar. The surroundings were familiar, but once that game started, it hit me: *This is a whole different deal. I'm in the NFL now. These are men I'm playing against.* They handled us, 20–6, and were on their way to a Super Bowl title.

I was in for more surprises after our third game. The Pittsburgh Steelers beat us, 40–28. Two days later, I learned that Archie Manning and our tight end, future Hall of Famer Dave Casper, had been traded to the Minnesota Vikings for a pair of draft choices. Considering how upbeat we all felt after the Green Bay game, it was a lesson in how quickly things can change in the NFL.

I soon discovered how quickly life can change as well. At the time, Carrie and I were renting an apartment in Houston. That evening, my dad called us at the apartment. I knew Mom had been dealing with some back pain and had gone into the hospital to get it checked out right before I left for training camp. Now the results of those tests were in, and they were a surprise to everyone: Mom had cancer.

I talked on the phone with both Dad and Mom. They were optimistic about it. They expected to beat it. I didn't know anything about cancer. I was concerned but not panicked. *Mom's been sick before*, I thought. *She'll do whatever it takes to get well.*

●　　●　　●

The Oilers' fortunes did not improve over the next several weeks. Ed Biles resigned after we lost to Denver and dropped to 0–6 on the season. It was the team's thirteenth consecutive defeat dating back to the year before. Biles was replaced by defensive coordinator Chuck Studley.

Our record was 0–10 when we hosted Detroit on November 13. The 5–5 Lions were favored by six points. My clearest memory from that game is Lions running back Billy Sims jumping into the air on a rush and hitting our cornerback, Steve Brown, with a karate kick to the chest. You can still catch it on YouTube. But for once, we were the better team. Earl Campbell rushed for 107 yards, Oliver Luck (father of quarterback Andrew Luck) threw a pair of touchdown passes, and we beat Detroit, 27–17. I finally had my first NFL victory.

Two weeks later, we traveled to Tampa Bay. Both of our teams had records of 1–11. The media dubbed our matchup the Repus Bowl (*repus* is *super* spelled backward). *Sports Illustrated*'s Steve Wulf wrote, "Yes, this was the Small One, the battle of the beatens, the movable object meeting the resistible force. There were only tomorrows. When these two teams get together, nothing can happen. This game was for a marble." I remember some of the Tampa fans had bags over their heads. I had to laugh when I saw guys walking around the stadium with a banner that read, "We Told Our Wives We Went to a Professional Football Game."

We were two bad teams. Naturally, Tampa Bay beat us, 33–24. I was learning about the highs and lows of the NFL. This was definitely one of the lows.

I was looking forward to our second-to-last game of the season, however. We hosted Cleveland in my second NFL matchup against my brother. I was looking for redemption after whiffing on that block and losing to the Browns in our first game. Even more, I was excited that the whole family would be there. Carrie and I had just moved into a house in a Houston suburb and HBO was coming in to do a television special on the Matthews family. The Browns allowed Bruz to visit us the night before to participate in the HBO piece. Mom's brother drove up from Corpus Christi. And of course, Mom and Dad flew in. I hadn't seen Mom since before training camp.

When she arrived, I was shocked. I knew she'd been going through chemotherapy treatments but I still did not expect to see such a change. She had lost her long blonde hair and wore a wig. She was physically weak and had to be transported in a wheelchair. It was hard to believe that this was the same woman who only recently had been an excellent golfer, years ago winning some matches at a North Carolina country club. Golf was something she and I had shared and enjoyed, once playing sixteen or seventeen days in a row. Now she looked like she'd have trouble riding in a golf cart.

That weekend, though, Mom as usual made sure the focus stayed on the entire family, not her. Even though she was feeling terrible, she talked about how excited she was to be there and never complained or left the room when the HBO filming went late. The next day, Mom and Dad watched me play as a pro for the first time. Even better, at least from my perspective, we beat the Browns, 34–27. Earl Campbell ran for 130 yards and Tim Smith had a huge day at receiver, gaining 150 yards and catching the winning touchdown pass in the fourth quarter from Oliver Luck. Though he finished on the losing side, Bruz had a pair of quarterback sacks against us. All in all, it was a good day for the Matthews family.

We lost our last game, and the final game in the history of the Colts franchise in Baltimore, 20–10. We finished my first NFL season with a record of 2–14. In many ways the year had been a disaster, yet I was optimistic about the future. We had a lot of talented young players and a stockpile of draft choices. I was looking forward to being part of a team that could only get better.

A dark cloud hung over all that optimism, however. Mom was not getting better. Carrie and I were back in our condo in California for Christmas and saw that Mom was declining. The chemotherapy was taking a toll and the cancer was progressing. Mom was sedated most of the time over the next several weeks. She never recovered. At three in the morning on March 8, 1984, Dad called. At age fifty-six, Mom had passed away.

Mom was the heart and soul of our family. She'd always cared and always encouraged me and my brothers and sister. Growing up, if I ever wanted to ask a girl out or had a problem, I would talk to her and walk away feeling like I could take care of it. She'd always steered me in the right direction. When she heard that I'd gotten in trouble for something like talking in class, she'd say, "You shouldn't be doing that, Bruce. You're too nice a boy for that." It was a way to get her message across while still being positive. Like most moms, she'd been my champion from the day I was born. I couldn't believe she was gone. I was so blessed to have her in my life. The void she left is still there today.

Losing my mom reminded me that life is short for all of us and that we should cherish those we love while we can. Taken by itself, that philosophy might sound a little trite and hopeless. But I had just discovered something that put it into perspective—a hope more powerful than anything I'd experienced before.

9

BIGGER THAN THE GAME

I am the way and the truth and the life.
No one comes to the Father except through me.

JOHN 14:6

ALL MY LIFE, IT SEEMED, I'D been working on a checklist. Once I marked all the boxes on my list, I made a new list. In high school, my checklist included "make the varsity, become a starter, earn all-league honors." After high school, it was "get a scholarship from USC, make the travel team, start, be named an All-American, get drafted by the NFL, find the right girl, get married."

By the time I joined the Oilers, I had mentally checked off nearly all my boxes. In many ways, I had achieved everything I'd hoped for. I was making good money as a professional football player. I was married to the girl of my dreams. The future was bright.

At the beginning of my rookie year, I expected to feel a sense of fulfillment, of having arrived. My philosophy had always been that if I kept working my list, I'd be happy. Yet something was missing. My accomplishments seemed hollow. I was a success in my field and believed I was generally a good person. But I couldn't shake the feeling that there had to be more to life than moving three-hundred-pound bodies six inches.

All of that was in the back of my mind when I showered after our Friday practice before our opening game against Green Bay. Through the sound of water cascading over my head, I heard the familiar voice of Mike "Mongo" Stensrud, our nose tackle, over the intercom: "Hey, we're going to have Bible study in fifteen minutes in the defense meeting room."

I knew that the Oilers, like the rest of the NFL, had a team chaplain. I also knew that Stensrud was a Christian. *Maybe I should check that out sometime. Maybe those guys would have something to say about this empty feeling.*

We'd gone to church sporadically when I was a kid. The services seemed pretty regimented and designed for grown-ups. I mostly fidgeted in the pews. Out of boredom, I sometimes opened up a Bible and looked for the words in red. It seemed random to me—I didn't know then that those were the words Jesus spoke. I can't say I walked out of those services feeling overly inspired.

Faith wasn't something our family talked about much. I believed in God and tried to live right. I knew there was more to faith than that, but I was too invested in the things I wanted to do to take time to investigate it. Carrie, on the other hand, grew up going to church regularly. She pledged her life to Christ at a Campus Crusade meeting when she was fifteen and learned how to recite all the titles of the books in the Bible. Carrie definitely knew more about faith than I did. But neither of us was very committed to spiritual development in college. We were both pretty ignorant in terms of what God was really about.

On that Friday at the beginning of my rookie year, I was nearly dressed in the locker room when Mongo walked past and looked at me. "Hey," he said, "you comin' to the study?"

Stensrud was a veteran and I was a rookie. I didn't want to disappoint him. And I *was* interested in finding out what these guys were up to. I decided "sometime" had just become "right now."

"Sure," I said. "I'll be there in a minute."

The defense meeting area was a large room filled with those chairs you see in classrooms with a desk that can flip up or down. When I walked in, the room had been partitioned by a divider. In the middle of our section, a handful of chairs had been arranged in a circle. I figured out that the tall man I didn't recognize was the team chaplain.

Greg Headington turned out to be a soft-spoken, down-to-earth guy with a sense of humor. He wasn't stuffy or churchy, which appealed to me. More important, he spoke from the Bible and how it related to the life issues my teammates and I were dealing with on a day-to-day basis—how to treat your wife, what to do when your marriage feels shaky, how to handle fear of injury. I don't remember now what he talked about that first day, but it got my attention enough to want to go back. I also was impressed that the players who attended, usually no more than five to ten guys, would talk openly about what they were struggling with. I began attending the Friday Bible studies and Sunday morning chapels Greg hosted for the Oilers.

I also watched Mongo Stensrud. Like most defensive linemen, Stensrud was big and strong, six foot five and 280 pounds. He was a clean-shaven, corn-fed white guy from Iowa who'd joined the Oilers during the "Luv Ya Blue" era. He had a reputation as a wild man, always ready to party. He soon confirmed in our Bible study meetings that the rumors about his past were mostly true—during his early years in Houston, his marriage had apparently been on the brink of divorce. But then he'd found Jesus and his focus and life changed.

What I found interesting was that even though Mongo's character had changed, his overall personality hadn't. He was still a goofball between plays in practice. You had to be careful walking back to the huddle—he'd flick you in a sensitive spot if you weren't looking. Once, he said to me, "Hey, let's get into a fight after this play."

"What?" I said. "What are you talking about?"

Sure enough, after the next play ended, we were in the middle of the field, wrestling. Mongo did crazy stuff like that all the time. But once the ball was snapped, he went after it. Since he was a nose tackle and I was on the offensive line, we battled each other in practice every day. He definitely didn't take it easy on me, which I respected.

For some reason, Mongo and Gregg Bingham, a couple of veterans on defense, hung out often with Mike Munchak and me those first couple of years. As I spent time with Mongo, I saw that his passion for the Lord was real. He had a purpose and a peace that I wanted.

The more I went to the Bible studies and chapel and talked with Greg, the more I realized that Jesus was the answer to the emptiness I'd been feeling. I started reading the Bible from the beginning. Though that generated a ton of questions, the story of God's people and love for each of us made sense to me. *Yeah, this is true,* I thought. *I know this is true.*

I don't remember the exact words or moment, but sometime during that rookie year I prayed to Jesus, professing my belief in Him and asking Him to forgive my sins and direct my steps. I was still an immature believer, really just scratching the surface of my understanding of what it all meant. But I'd begun the journey to a spiritual relationship that would become the foundation of my life.

It wasn't as if I experienced a sudden, dramatic transformation. From the outside, the shift was barely noticeable. But as Carrie can explain, over time she began to detect that my deepening faith was leading to a few important and positive changes.

I thought it was great that Bruce attended the team Bible studies. It was wonderful that the Oilers made that available to the players. He would come home and talk about some of their discussions and what he was learning. I'd always thought he was a Christian, but he'd never made it official, so of course I was thrilled when he told me he'd invited Christ into his life.

It wasn't that he suddenly figured out he'd been doing everything all wrong. We were already going to church every Sunday and we already had a fully committed marriage. But there were some subtle differences. He started sharing more with me in general and specifically what he was learning about the Lord. It took a few years, but he became more helpful around the house, doing the dishes or offering to go to the grocery store. They were small things, but I appreciated them. And he began an insatiable quest for biblical knowledge. He became a font of spiritual information.

The biggest change I saw was an ever-growing peace. Bruce had a stressful job, but I could tell that his developing faith gave him new strength and comfort. And that gave me even more peace about our relationship because I think it takes three. It has to be you, your spouse, and the Lord for a marriage to work well. It's not that I ever had any worries about our marriage or that the idea of divorce was even mentioned. When we said at our wedding, "to have and to hold for better or for worse," we meant it. But we've had our struggles and trials like any couple. I don't know how couples handle it if they don't have the Lord. I've seen husbands and wives driven apart by their differences, yet when we face trials it usually seems to drive us closer. I give our relationship with the Lord all the credit for that.

● ● ●

I had more new relationships to develop during those early years in our marriage. The first began on March 16, 1985, when Carrie gave birth to our first child, Steven Bruce Matthews.

Carrie and I both wanted a large family. I knew how important family was to me and how much I loved having a sister and brothers. Carrie and I each grew up with four siblings. Carrie actually wanted eight kids when she was in high school, but figured the boys would take off once they heard that, so she cut the number to six. I really looked forward to being a parent.

It was exciting when Steven was born. I couldn't believe I was a dad. But it was suddenly humbling and left me feeling a little panicked. We were responsible for this little baby—just us. On the trip home from the hospital, I drove more carefully than I did on my driver's test. Was I equipped to be a father? Even after nine months of getting ready for this moment, I felt totally unprepared.

When we got home, we closed the shades and turned the lights off so Steven could sleep. Then I called my dad. "No, what are you doing?" he said. "You *want* the light and noise so he doesn't sleep all day and stay awake all night."

"Okay, that makes sense," I said. Where was the instruction

manual for parenting anyway? Fortunately, Carrie filled in where I lacked. She was and is an awesome mom.

A year and a half later, Carrie was expecting again. I wasn't quite as nervous as with the first pregnancy, but I was anxious in another way. In October 1986, I began having trouble with nagging sciatic nerve pain. It wasn't bad enough to make me miss practice or games, but I could barely handle sitting down for more than thirty seconds at a time.

I hoped the pain would disappear after the season ended, but that didn't happen. Then one night I tried doing a light workout. It left me hunched over—I couldn't stand straight.

Our baby was due in late February 1987, but on February 4 Carrie went into labor. I wasn't much help at the hospital—I was lying on the floor trying to relieve my back pain. Even without my assistance, Kevin James soon joined the Matthews family. My back issues threatened to put a damper on the day for me. In fact, when we left the hospital, I was the one in the wheelchair holding our new baby while Carrie steered us, instead of the other way around.

But nothing could take away from the blessings God was giving me. At home, it was such a joy just to be with Carrie and Steven and watch Kevin as he wriggled, cried, laughed, and slept in his crib. I had a wonderful, expanding family and I was growing closer to Jesus. These were the relationships that mattered. This was what would last for eternity.

That empty feeling? The Lord was filling it up, not with my achievements on the football field, but with family and peace and love. And that was just fine with me.

10

WITH ALL YOUR HEART

So whether you eat or drink or whatever you do,
do it all for the glory of God.

1 CORINTHIANS 10:31

JUST AS MY FAITH GRADUALLY GREW stronger during the mid-to-late eighties, so did the quality of the teams I played on in the NFL. After that 2–14 performance my rookie year, the Oilers finished 3–13 in 1984. It was hardly a great leap forward, but we added an important piece to the puzzle before the season: quarterback Warren Moon.

In 1978, Warren came out of the University of Washington and went undrafted by the NFL. He joined Edmonton in the Canadian Football League, where he led the Eskimos to five consecutive Grey Cup victories and was named the league's Most Outstanding Player in 1983. With his talents finally recognized, Warren decided to switch to the NFL. Houston won a bidding war for his rights and signed him for the next season.

Warren didn't exactly blow the league away during his first three years with us, but you could tell right away he had the ability. He worked hard, was always professional, and threw the tightest spiral I'd ever seen. When he released the ball, his index finger made a little popping noise. I heard that sound a lot over the ten years Warren played for the Oilers. He retired in 2000 after additional stints in Minnesota, Seattle, and Kansas City. If you combined his CFL and NFL statistics, Warren Moon had more pass attempts, pass completions, passing yards, and touchdowns than anyone when he left the game. He's in the Hall of Fame in both leagues.

But when Warren joined the Oilers, he had to adjust to the NFL and get to know his new team. I had some adjustments to make myself. During our 1984 minicamp, the Oilers asked me to move from right guard to center. I still remembered my dad's advice to follow what the coaches thought best. If it would help the team, I was all for it. Then the Oilers made a midseason trade for Raiders' center Jim Romano. Once Jim was ready to start for us, in week ten against Pittsburgh, they moved me back to right guard.

We'd drafted Nebraska's Dean Steinkuhler with the second overall pick before the season. Dean was our starting right tackle and a real stud. Houston had put a big emphasis on having a quality offensive line, but our new and improved lineup with Romano didn't last long. In that Steelers' game, Steinkuhler's knee got torn up. He missed the rest of the season and all of the next year. Although Dean had a good career, playing seven seasons, he was never the same after that injury.

With Dean out, the coaches asked me to move to my third position in 1984, right tackle. I learned a new set of pass-block assignments and started the last six games. Other than allowing a sack to the

Jets' Mark Gastineau, who was on his way to an NFL record twenty-two that season, I played pretty well.

In 1985, we raised our stock a bit more, going from three wins to five. I started all sixteen games at right tackle and was named as an alternate to the Pro Bowl. Our record was the same the next year. Harvey Salem, our left tackle, wanted out of Houston and was traded to the Lions at the beginning of the 1986 season. You can guess what that meant for me—another position switch. I started every game at left tackle. Except for the day in Cleveland when Bruz beat me for a sack, I think I had a good season.

In four years, I'd started at four different positions on the offensive line. I'm not sure that anybody's done that before or since in the modern NFL.

The 1987 NFL season highlighted a lingering dispute between league players and owners. The players had gone on strike in 1982, before eventually signing a collective bargaining agreement without achieving any of their primary goals. That agreement expired in summer 1987. Now, the players again were talking strike. The big issues were the idea of tying player salaries to league revenue and player freedom. At the time, if a player felt the team holding his rights wasn't offering him a fair contract, he could either sign anyway, hold out for more money, or retire. Players had no avenue for taking their services to another team.

To me and a lot of my teammates, it felt like a one-sided system in favor of the owners. And, that summer, it affected me directly.

The four-year contract I'd signed with Houston as a rookie had expired after the 1986 season. The Oilers' new offer seemed far too low to me. I felt I'd done everything the organization asked of me, and performed well despite almost unprecedented position changes. It was true that I hadn't yet been named to a Pro Bowl, but I believed I would have if the team had left me at one position. I thought I should be paid at that level. The Oilers disagreed.

My negotiations with the team moved in a direction I hadn't anticipated or wanted. On the advice of my agent, I held out for a better deal. I didn't report to training camp. I missed the preseason. Then I found myself at home in California, watching the Oilers host the Los Angeles Rams on television in our season opener. *Are you kidding me?* I thought. *They're playing without me.* The Oilers won too. That humbled me. Looking back today, it's almost funny. I guess I had a pretty high opinion of myself then.

I wasn't the only player trying to fight for better pay or other changes. After the second week of the season, the members of the NFL Players Association went on strike. The league responded by canceling the third week of the season and hiring replacement players: guys who had been cut from teams previously, had retired, or had otherwise played the game but weren't good enough for the real NFL. For the next three weeks, those replacements—along with some NFL players who disagreed with the strike—played games that the league counted.

Meanwhile, I sued the league. My lawsuit said that the NFL and Oilers, in violation of antitrust law, had conspired to prevent me from negotiating or signing with other league teams. I argued that since the collective bargaining agreement had expired and I didn't have a contract, I should be declared a free agent. I felt it was the only option I had left.

During the strike, NFL owners showed no sign of compromise. After week six, the Players Association caved in, ending the strike without winning any concessions. About a week later, the Oilers traded for Raiders tackle Bruce Davis, an obvious sign they were preparing to move on without me. The next day, the courts ruled against me in my lawsuit, saying that I was not a free agent.

The Oilers organization and NFL owners had triumphed on all fronts. That night, I took a red-eye flight to Houston, arriving about five thirty in the morning. I took a cab to the general manager's office. With my figurative tail between my legs, I said I would accept the team's last contract offer and sign a contract.

Though we lost those battles, the owners probably hurt themselves in the long run with their tough stance. Two years later, the NFL Players Association disbanded, so players could pursue their battles in court. That led to the NFL losing antitrust protections and to the system of limited free agency and greater financial benefits that players have today. As you might expect, my sympathy was with the players on this one. They're the ones that fans pay money to watch and that risk debilitating injury every time they step on the field. In my opinion, they deserve a significant share of all the revenue the league takes in.

When I reported to the team in November 1987, I was bitter, angry, and stressed about the way my situation had turned out. Right after I signed my contract, I went to our practice facility. No one knew I was coming. The rest of the guys had just walked onto the practice field. I dressed quickly and joined them.

I'd been working out but I was not in game shape. The coaches put me on the so-called "show" team with the backup players who imitated our upcoming opponent—that week, the 49ers—and prepared our starters for the weekend game. I was still fuming over everything as I faced off against our top defensive players.

One of those guys was defensive tackle Ray Childress. I'd had a few minor skirmishes with Ray before. It can happen when two guys are going hard against each other, even in practice and even if they're on the same team. But that wasn't my role in that moment. I was supposed to be demonstrating the 49er formations to help our guys get ready to play. Instead, however, I just wanted to hit people.

Not surprisingly, Ray didn't appreciate my "enthusiasm." Pretty soon we were shoving each other. Then we were grabbing each other's face masks, trying to raise the other guy's neck into an uncomfortable position. Then guys on both sides of the ball moved in to break us up.

I don't blame Ray for reacting how he did—I'd have done the same if it had been the other way around. But a strange thing happened in that moment. That brief fight was a release of all the tension and anxiety that had built up inside me. *This is cool,* I thought. *I'm back where I belong.* The longer the practice went, the better I felt. It was refreshing to be tired physically and unburdened mentally at the end of it.

I was reminded that day how much I enjoyed just being with the guys and playing football. The business side of the NFL was a necessary evil, but I didn't have to let it infect my passion for playing. Football was a game, one I'd always loved. It was time to get back to seeing it that way.

I also began reflecting more on what my faith meant in all of this. The Bible verse that seemed relevant was Colossians 3:23: "Whatever you do, work at it with all your heart, as working for the Lord, not for men." This wasn't just about football. I'd been blessed with a certain ability and the opportunity to use it. I was tired of trying to figure out what I deserved to be paid and what people in the Houston organization and NFL thought of me. Forget all this, I thought. I'm going to play harder than ever. I'm going all out, full speed.

The events of that year and the perspective they gave me combined to make me more determined than ever to take my game to another level. For all I knew, every upcoming play could be my last. I would not take my career for granted. I wouldn't say I was reckless, but from that point on I played with fierce intensity on every down.

If NFL teams thought I was a good player before, they hadn't seen anything yet.

11

BROTHERS IN ARMS

As iron sharpens iron, so one man sharpens another.

PROVERBS 27:17

My ATTITUDE WAS NOT THE ONLY change for the 1987 season. When I'd reported to our minicamp in May, I'd met our new quarterbacks coach, June Jones. He and head coach Jerry Glanville were installing a new offense they called "Red Gun," which contained elements of the Run-and-Shoot system they'd introduced as coaches at Portland State University. It meant lining up at times with four wideouts, a pass-first approach that flooded the field with small but speedy receivers. The new style was interesting, but it's easy for an offense to look great on paper and in practice. I wanted to see how it worked in real games.

Once I rejoined the team, I got my answer: Red Gun was a success. We moved up and down the field far more easily than I'd ever experienced in Houston. Our record was 5–2 when I rejoined the Oilers. We already had as many wins as we'd notched in any season since I'd been in the NFL. Not surprisingly, the team was more confident. Instead of "I hope we win today," the attitude was, "We're going to win this one."

Part of this change was because of the new offense and how it capitalized on Warren Moon's ability to read defenses and make accurate passes. Part of it was the talent the organization had assembled. But another important factor was that so many of us had grown up together in the NFL. There was a sense of familiarity, camaraderie, and trust that doesn't always exist in professional sports. We enjoyed playing together on the field and being together off it.

For me, the biggest example of that camaraderie was my best friend and new roommate on road trips, Mike Munchak. I'd first seen "Munch" playing for Penn State back in the Fiesta Bowl my junior year at USC, but since we were both offensive linemen we didn't actually meet or cross paths on the field. I was barely aware of him. Then he was chosen eighth overall by the Oilers in the 1982 NFL draft. I remembered his name after that.

Once Houston drafted me the next year, I couldn't forget his name if I tried. Over and over, people kept saying, "Mike Munchak, he's such a great player" and "You have to meet him." But I didn't meet him. The league didn't have a big offseason program like it does now, so there was no opportunity then. He wasn't at the Oilers minicamp because he was on his honeymoon. Then I missed the first twelve days of training camp because of my holdout. Once I did arrive, the rest of the players had that beaten down, walking-dead look. They were just trying to get through the practices. No one was talking to anybody.

It wasn't until a charity event after our preseason game against the Cowboys that I actually had the chance to talk with my heralded teammate. I discovered we both had similar interests, including TV shows: *Magnum, P.I.*; *Simon & Simon*; and *Knots Landing*. We were similar in other ways, too; we were both quiet and both passionate about doing well. It also helped that Carrie and Mike's wife, Marci, hit it off. We started spending more time with the Munchaks and getting to know them.

Munch and I argued about everything. California was better than Pennsylvania. Penn State was better than USC. The Lakers were better than the Celtics. If he took one position, I took the other. We entertained ourselves that way. We also "entertained" after some of our games. We might go to a place where a band was playing. If I'd had a beer or two, Munch would whisper to someone in the band, "Hey, my buddy can sing a little Elvis." Soon, I'd be up with the band doing my impression of Elvis Presley singing "Heartbreak Hotel." My strategy as a performer was to hit it hard and fast, then get off the stage before the crowd realized what had happened. I'm not sure what the rest of the audience thought, but Munch always got a kick out of it.

As a player, Munch had strengths different from mine. I was probably the better athlete and faster runner. He was stronger. At six foot three and 281 pounds, he was shorter and thicker, with huge arms. My goal when I worked out with Munch was to outdo him lifting weights, but I never came close. His game was brute power. When Munch hit someone in the open field, that guy went flying.

A left guard, Munch made the Pro Bowl in both 1984 and 1985. It was a well-deserved honor and I was happy for him, but it made me want to do the same even more. In 1986 I played alongside Munch at left tackle until he got hurt. He dealt with injuries and played with pain that season and through much of his career, yet I never heard him complain. His approach inspired me to persevere through my own relatively minor aches and pains.

Munch inspired me in other ways. I was impressed with the way he carried himself. He wasn't one to brag or fill the air with empty words. When he talked, he cut to the chase. After his first daughter, Alex, was born in 1986, he was all about his family off the field. Extended family was important to him as well. Every year, Munch and his family planned a bus trip from his hometown of Scranton, Pennsylvania, to one of our away games in Pittsburgh or Cleveland. Maybe two hundred Munchak family members and friends would show up to watch us play. I wanted to be like that—to say something worth hearing when I opened my mouth and to reflect that kind of family commitment.

Most significant of all, Munch and I grew in our faith together. He started coming to the team Bible studies. We bounced questions and thoughts about God off each other.

I needed that sounding board. I'd begun meeting one-on-one with Greg Headington on our off day, Tuesday. I asked a lot of questions about the Bible. Greg asked me probing questions about my beliefs and life that had a way of getting to the core of whatever we were discussing. It wasn't easy for me. Like most guys, I'd grown up believing that real men don't talk about their feelings and if they have a problem, they fix it themselves. Opening up, being vulnerable, trusting other guys—that wasn't me. Greg challenged me on that pretty quickly.

"God wants us to step out in faith," he said. "He wants us to talk about our doubts or whatever we need help with, get out of our comfort zone, and serve Him. I try to put myself in at least one uncomfortable spot every day."

What, are you crazy? I thought. *I don't want any discomfort in my life.* I soon learned, however, that God doesn't want us to focus on our comfort or our shortcomings. This really hit home when I read the story about Moses resisting God's command to lead the Hebrews out of Egypt, because he was "slow of speech and tongue." I can relate to how Moses felt. I'm much more comfortable behind the scenes and almost always feel anxious about getting up and speaking to a crowd. But God said, "Who gave man his mouth? Is it not I, the Lord? Now go; I will help you speak and will teach you what to say" (Exodus 4:10–12). We aren't supposed to be comfortable in this life. We are supposed to trust and serve God wherever He leads us.

Just talking about those challenges and discoveries with Munch was a way of stretching past my comfort zone. It was great to share my spiritual journey with a fellow believer and friend.

Munch's presence in those early years in the NFL, and in many years to follow, was important to me. I'm not sure he's aware of how much it meant. Every man needs male friends, guys he can share problems with who don't judge, yet are willing to speak up when he's going down the wrong path. The Bible says, "One who has unreliable friends soon comes to ruin, but there is a friend who sticks closer than a brother" (Proverbs 18:24). More than anyone in my life, that friend was Mike Munchak.

Even though the Oilers were more confident in 1987, we still stumbled late in the season, losing three times in November. Going into our second-to-last game of the season, our record was 7–6. We had to defeat both the Steelers and Cincinnati Bengals, two teams we'd struggled against, to make the playoffs for the first time in my career. Fortunately, both games were in the Astrodome.

The Pittsburgh contest was a battle. Even though the Steelers had outgained us in yardage, we were up by a point in the fourth quarter, 17–16. Then Warren hit Drew Hill with a thirty-yard touchdown pass, Hill's second long score of the game. We had the victory, 24–16.

The following week, Jerry Glanville had T-shirts made for the team. They featured an armadillo—I'm still not entirely sure what that signified—and the slogan, "Let's Get Paid." We needed just one more triumph against the Bengals. We scored three touchdowns in the first half, two by rookie Alonzo Highsmith, his only scores of the season. We were shut out in the second half. But those three early touchdowns were just enough. Our defense came through and we held on to win 21–17. I wore my T-shirt proudly after that.

Those two victories showed the emerging character of our team. It was great to know we were finally in the playoffs. I felt as if we'd made a statement: "The Oilers have arrived." Even though we were new to the postseason, I was optimistic. I believed we could get on a roll and go all the way to the Super Bowl.

We hosted the Seattle Seahawks in the American Football Conference wild card game on January 3, 1988. As usual, I went onto the field before most of the players to practice with the field goal and punt units. The Astrodome was a fun place to play. The fans were enthusiastic and loud—once they got going, the noise bounced off the walls and roof inside the dome and could be a major distraction for the visiting team. On this day, I saw that fans were already arriving and that all the A-list people were there, including NBC announcers Marv Albert and Joe Namath.

This is for real, I thought. The atmosphere was electric.

Seattle scored first after we threw an interception on the opening drive. We responded with thirteen consecutive points. Both Munch and I were having strong games. During one play, Munch ripped the jersey off outspoken and controversial rookie linebacker Brian Bosworth. The "Boz" returned to the game later wearing a different number.

We were up, 20–13, going into the fourth quarter and were out-gaining the Seahawks, but we couldn't put them away. Our kicker, Tony Zendejas, booted a ball that hit the uprights and bounced back on a fifty-two-yard field goal attempt. Then Tony missed another kick from twenty-nine yards. With 1:47 left to play, Seattle got the ball and drove eighty yards. Steve Largent caught a twelve-yard touchdown pass with twenty-six seconds left in the game. My first NFL playoff game was going to overtime.

I was confident we'd find a way to score and win the game—our offensive line was consistently pushing back their defense. The Seahawks won the coin flip and got the ball first, but we forced them to punt. Just as I predicted, we drove into their territory. Eight minutes into the extra period, Tony lined up for another field goal attempt, this one from forty-two yards away. I snapped the ball, holder Jeff Gossett caught and positioned it, and Tony's kick was true. I had my first playoff victory.

Our next playoff opponent was Denver in Mile High Stadium. I believed we matched up well with the Broncos, but a terrible start doomed us. In hindsight, the opening game plan designed by our coaches might have been too risky.

Jerry Glanville was just as colorful as our old coach, Bum Phillips, but in different ways. Glanville was known for leaving tickets for Elvis at the Oilers' box office—even though Elvis had been dead for a decade—and for firing up opposing teams and coaches with some of his comments. He once taunted a Bengals punter and had long-running feuds with Bengals coach Sam Wyche and Steelers coach Chuck Noll.

Against the Broncos, Glanville cemented his reputation as a gambler. Our defense stopped Denver on its opening drive and we took over in a tough spot, on our five-yard line. Our first play lost a yard. Our next one was a trick play called "Stagger Lee," after an old country blues song about gamblers. Unfortunately, the trick was on us. Running back Mike Rozier lined up wide left behind three blockers. We were so backed up that Rozier was in the end zone when Warren threw him a lateral. The play should have worked—Denver had only two defenders in position to stop Rozier. But Mike couldn't handle the ball, the Broncos recovered, and they scored a touchdown soon after. On our next drive, an interception led to another Denver touchdown.

We couldn't overcome that miserable beginning. We trailed 24–3 at halftime and even though we finished with more total yards than the Broncos, they beat us, 34–10.

Losing that game hurt. Our year was suddenly over. But at the same time, it felt like a beginning. We had a strong and talented core of guys who were just coming into their prime. With the season on the line in the final two regular-season games and again in the play-offs, we'd provided a glimpse of the team we could be—tough, physical, relentless. I knew we'd be back in the playoffs and that the rest of the NFL would have to reckon with us.

I was proud of my team. These guys were my brothers in arms, teammates I was ready to go to war with. I couldn't wait for the next season to begin.

12

DEFEATS AND DELIGHTS

You make known to me the path of life;
you will fill me with joy in your presence.

PSALM 16:11

IF I'D KNOWN IN 1988 ALL the ups and downs the next six years would bring both professionally and personally, I wonder if I would have approached my circumstances differently. I'm sure it's best that I didn't know. I wouldn't have believed I was ready to face them. I was about to experience some of the deepest disappointments and greatest joys of my life.

That spring brought one of the joys. Carrie was pregnant with our third baby and, though we would have been happy either way, after two boys we were ready for a daughter. Marilyn Elizabeth was born April 14, just two days after the Munchaks' second child, Julie. Marilyn was our "Cocoa Puff" baby—instead of being blond and fair like Carrie and our first two boys, she had dark hair, brown eyes, and a dark complexion like me. My wife says we can thank my contract holdout nine months earlier for our first girl.

I was also thankful for the Oilers' performance in 1988. We finished 10–6, reaching double figures in wins for the first time in my pro career. In addition, I played on *Monday Night Football* for the first time. It was exciting to be on the nationally televised broadcast and it was satisfying to beat Bruz's Browns in that game, 24–17. In later years, though, the thrill of playing on Monday night began to wear off. I always enjoyed being in a featured game, but I didn't care for the disruption in my schedule. It meant an extra day to prepare for our opponent that week and one less day to prepare the next week. I appreciated having my routine.

We beat the Browns again in the first round of the 1988 playoffs, 24–23. The next round at Buffalo was a different story, however. Someone rolled my ankle during a play in the second quarter. It swelled up so much that I felt like I was playing with a peg leg. Even worse, we couldn't seem to make the plays we needed to against a strong Bills defense. We managed only one field goal over the first three quarters and got beat 17–10.

I was disappointed to miss the opportunity to keep playing but pleased to be honored after the season. I was chosen for the first of my fourteen consecutive Pro Bowls and named to the first of my seven All-Pro first teams. That took a bit of the sting out of losing.

The next season was memorable for a pair of games against the Steelers. The first was a November matchup in the Astrodome. We had an excellent punter, Greg Montgomery, who would become an All-Pro in 1993. Greg had already tweaked his hamstring sometime before that day. Normally, during pregame warmups, I snapped the ball to him for twenty to twenty-five practice kicks. But on this day, Greg walked off the field after just two kicks. His hamstring was hurting.

Uh-oh. Guess who the team's backup punter was?

I'd always seen myself as an all-around athlete. Going back to high school, I'd enjoyed working out with the kickers and punters and asking questions about their technique. I kicked with them occasionally and became a decent punter. On the Oilers, I challenged other guys to a game I called "Punt Master," which was a one-on-one field position battle to see who was the best punter.

There's a big difference, though, between messing around on the practice field and punting in front of thousands of people in an NFL game. I couldn't imagine doing it against the Steelers. I already had my hands taped and knee braces on. What if I whiffed? Yet, as Greg headed for the locker room, I heard the special teams coach say, "All right, Bruce, get back there and try a few. You've got to be ready to go."

I was never so nervous in my life.

Fortunately, Greg felt good enough or got taped up enough to go for it in the game. He managed fine and we beat the Steelers easily that day. You won't find many linemen standing back there in punt formation in the NFL—I've never seen it—but the world almost got to witness it that afternoon in the Astrodome. I'm kind of grateful it didn't happen.

I felt less grateful after our final game against Pittsburgh that year. We'd finished the season with a 9–7 record and again qualified for a wild card playoff game. We were seven-point favorites and had a seven-point lead in the fourth quarter, but the Steelers scored to send the game into overtime and won on a fifty-yard field goal by Gary Anderson. Once again, we'd let an opportunity slide past.

As disappointed as I was about the loss, our owner, Bud Adams, must have been even more upset. He fired Jerry Glanville. Jerry was a good coach, but his confrontational style and conflicts with opposing coaches weren't always helpful. The Bengals had embarrassed us, 61–7, in the second-to-last game of the season. They were driven by their hatred of Glanville. You don't want to be the guy who's saying or doing things that give the other team extra motivation.

Our new coach for my eighth year in the NFL was Jack Pardee from the University of Houston. He brought with him the offensive style we'd partially utilized in the past and that was perfect for Warren Moon—the Run and Shoot. It meant we nearly always lined up with just one running back and four wide receivers and nearly always threw the ball.

As an offensive lineman, there's nothing like running the ball at a defense that knows what's coming and still can't stop you. I had that experience at USC and loved it. It was the opposite of the Run and Shoot, as we were one-dimensional with our passing. The challenge was that the defensive linemen we had to block knew we'd be passing nearly every down, so they could charge at us from the snap to try to take down the quarterback.

Yet the new offense worked, which was the bottom line. Any offense is fun if it allows you to move downfield, score, and win. Warren started recording crazy passing numbers. Late in the season, we played in Kansas City's Arrowhead Stadium. It was raining and freezing, but Warren was on fire. He threw for three touchdowns and 527 yards, still the second-highest yardage total in NFL history.

In the next game, however—a loss to Cincinnati—Warren dislocated his thumb on his throwing hand. He was out for the year. We finished the regular season with a 9–7 record and 405 points, second in the league. Warren was named the Associated Press NFL Offensive Player of the Year. Once again, we qualified for a wild card playoff. And once again, we fell short. Without our top quarterback, the Bengals beat us convincingly, 41–14.

More highs followed by a disappointing low. It had become a disturbing pattern.

In 1991, after four years at right guard, I again changed positions. Bob Young, our offensive line coach, had moved me to center for the final regular-season game and playoff loss the year before. He felt it gave us a better chance to win. He decided to make the move permanent for the new season. I was anxious about the switch but also fired up since the coaches thought I could handle it and that it would improve the team.

At center, I had more responsibilities. I read the defense as I walked up to the line of scrimmage before a play and, depending on what I saw, gave a signal to our running back. If it was a nickel defense, for example—five defensive backs intended to counter a passing offense—I might make a fist, the signal for our running back to block any defenders who break through our protection where our quarterback was going. If the defense shifted or if I'd read it incorrectly, I might change the running back's assignment with another signal, such as an open hand.

Even after I was in my stance, my right hand on the ball, I might yell out more directions. For example, "Lenny!" meant that the left guard and I would throw a combination block on the defender across the line from us. In many ways, center was a complicated position to master, but after playing so many years I'd seen just about every imaginable defense and usually had a good idea as to what our opponent was up to.

I guess the coaches were right about the change, since our offense was prolific again in 1991. Warren was healthy all year and we went 11–5, winning the NFL's Central Division title for the first time. This time I was sure we'd go far in the playoffs.

Our first postseason game was another wild card matchup against the Jets. Our offense struggled to score, but fortunately our defense saved us. Bubba McDowell intercepted two passes inside our five-yard line. We held on to beat the Jets, 17–10, and advanced to play at Denver, the AFC West Division champions. Though the Broncos had taken us out four years earlier, I felt very confident this time. We were a stronger team than before and had blown the Broncos out in October.

My confidence appeared justified in the first half. We scored touchdowns on our first three possessions and could have had a fourth if not for an interception. Denver responded with its own touchdown late in the second quarter, but we still led 21–13 at halftime. We were moving the ball easily and for the most part, our defense was containing John Elway and the Broncos.

Our offense slowed down in the second half, but we still led 24–16 in the fourth quarter. Then Denver got a touchdown to cut our lead to a single point. We had a first down on Denver's thirty-four-yard line with 3:13 left to play, but a couple of penalties pushed us back. Greg Montgomery made his first punt of the day and it was a beauty. We downed the ball on the two-yard line. Denver had no time-outs and had to go ninety-eight yards in two minutes, seven seconds. We were in a great position.

The problem, though, was that Denver had Elway. He was already famous for his ninety-eight-yard, game-winning drive in the play-offs against the Browns five years earlier, a result that was devastating for my brother. Now Elway was trying to do it against me and my teammates.

Right away, the Broncos got room to operate with a twenty-two-yard completion to Michael Young. Four plays later we had them on the brink of defeat, fourth down and six yards to go, but Elway scrambled and barely made the first down. Three incompletions followed and we were again one play away from victory. But with fifty-nine seconds left, Elway eluded our rushers and threw a wobbly pass to Vance Johnson, who ran forty-four yards down the left sideline. With twenty seconds to go, the Broncos lined up for a twenty-eight-yard field goal. The snap was low, but holder Gary Kubiak got the ball in position a split second before Jeff Treadwell's foot met the ball. The kick was good.

Even down to that final minute, I was sure we'd win. Now I was in shock. Oh, my gosh, we're going to lose this game. I can't believe it.

After the game, I sat on the bus during the ride to the airport and tried to process my emotions. After working so hard all season to get to that point, it was heartbreaking to lose. When I was new to the league, I focused mostly on my own feelings. Now, after nine seasons in the NFL, I was more aware of the impact of a playoff loss on the whole team. Every season brought turnover in personnel. On Monday, we'd report to clear out our lockers and meet one last time with the coaches. This group of guys would never be together again.

The finality of it weighed on me. These opportunities didn't come often. We'd dropped some tough games in the past and would lose some big ones in the years ahead, but that last-gasp loss in Mile High Stadium was one of the toughest I ever experienced. After all the previous playoff disappointments and after leading the entire game, I didn't understand how we'd let another one slip away.

As much as that game hurt, it wasn't long before my perspective began to change. Carrie was pregnant again and on February 11, 1992, Jacob Thomas "Jake" Matthews joined the family. Once more, I was thrilled to be a new dad. Now a father of four kids, I was reminded that some things were more important than my football frustrations. My children didn't care if my team had scored fewer points than another team. They just wanted my love and attention. Enjoying time with my family was a blessing far beyond what I deserved.

We had a great team in 1992, maybe our best yet. Despite Warren missing five games because of a fractured left arm, we finished the season 10–6 and qualified for the playoffs for an NFL-leading sixth consecutive year. Warren returned for part of our last game and we beat Buffalo easily in the Dome, 27–3.

A week later, we were in Buffalo to play the Bills again in our annual wild card playoff game. The Bills had an excellent team—they'd made it to the Super Bowl the previous two seasons—but their quarterback, Jim Kelly, had been injured in that final regular-season game against us. Our prospects looked good.

By the end of the first half, our prospects had improved to near-certain victory. I'd never been involved in an NFL game where my team had so dramatically imposed its will on an opponent. Warren threw for four touchdowns, two of them to our All-Pro receiver

Haywood Jeffires, and we led 28–3. It was magical. I thought, *Let's just get this second half over with so we can get ready for the next playoff game.*

For Buffalo, it got even worse in the third quarter. On the Bills' opening drive, Bubba McDowell picked off a Reich pass and ran it back fifty-eight yards for another score. We led 35–3. Fans began to exit the stadium.

Buffalo finally showed some life, driving for a touchdown. With nothing to lose, the Bills tried an onside kick, recovered it, and scored a second touchdown. Now it was 35–17.

Between the halftime break and the crazy action in that third quarter, it felt like we hadn't played a down of offense for hours. I sat on our sideline bench with David Williams, our right tackle, and said, "Man, it would be wild if they came back and won this thing." I meant it as a joke, but as we looked at each other, I think we both realized it was actually possible.

That long break was the worst thing that could have happened to us. Suddenly our offense was out of sync. We punted after going nowhere and Buffalo scored on a twenty-six-yard pass to Andre Reed. On the second play of our next drive, the Bills intercepted. A minute later, Reed caught another touchdown pass, Buffalo's fourth of the quarter.

Suddenly, we were only up 35–31. The crowd in frozen Rich Stadium was going crazy and I was thinking, *We can't possibly blow this thing.*

Our magical, near-certain victory had turned into a nightmare. In the fourth quarter, we drove down the field and lined up for a field goal attempt to regain some momentum. But when I snapped the ball to our holder, Greg Montgomery, he fumbled the ball. No kick and Buffalo took over.

Frank Reich was having the game of his life. He drove the rejuvenated Bills down the field, helped by a thirty-five-yard run by Kenneth Davis. Moments later, from seventeen yards out, Reich hit Reed for yet another touchdown pass. With 3:08 to play, Buffalo led 38–35.

We actually rallied to tie the game on a field goal with twelve seconds left. *Okay*, I thought. *We've weathered the storm. We're going to laugh about this later. Now we've got this thing.* We even won the toss and started with the ball in overtime. But on third down, Warren's pass to Ernest Givins was intercepted on a play that could have been called pass interference. Three plays later, Doug Christie kicked a thirty-two-yard field goal and the celebration in Buffalo was on. It is still the largest deficit—thirty-two points—any team has overcome in league history. It's known in NFL lore simply as "The Comeback." In Houston, they called it "The Choke."

I had to give the Buffalo fans credit. Though some left, I was amazed at how many stayed and how loud they were. It was actually the least painful of my playoff losses because it was so surreal. It didn't seem like it was really happening.

Every year around playoff time, one of the networks replays the game on television. To this day, every time I watch the first half, I'm certain we're going to win.

The surreal didn't stop with The Comeback. It extended to the entire next season. I've never experienced a crazier year.

We rarely interacted with the Oilers owner, Bud Adams. Occasionally he came into the locker room to congratulate us after a win, but we never saw him before the season. Except in 1993. He addressed the team at training camp. "Next year," he said, "this team will be broken up because of the new salary cap." The NFL and players union had signed off on a new bargaining agreement that included more open free agency and a limit on team salaries. Since we had several high-priced veterans, the message was that some of us would have to go. The 1993 season was our last chance to win with the talent the Oilers had assembled. The pressure was on.

You could say we didn't respond well. We dropped four of our first five games. It was so bad that to shake things up, the coaches benched Warren for the next game at New England in favor of backup Cody Carlson. Then Cody got hurt running for a touchdown and Warren was back in there. Warren was always a competitor, but he had an extra edge to him that day. He threw for a pair of touchdowns and we beat the Patriots, 28–14.

Despite the win and Warren's resurgence, we had a controversy. On the day before the game, the wife of my fellow lineman, David Williams, went into labor and had a baby. Everyone was healthy, but David chose to stay in Houston with his family and miss the Patriots game. I understood being there for the birth of his first child—that's a huge moment—but once that was taken care of, I felt his next obligation was to his teammates. Bud Adams fined David and said he had "misplaced priorities," which set off a media firestorm dubbed "Babygate." Since David's locker was next to mine, I had to deal with an overflow crowd of reporters when he came back. It was a distraction.

We put that craziness behind us and started winning. When we nipped Bruz's Browns on December 12, 19–17, we'd won eight straight. But those achievements felt hollow a couple of days later. In the early morning hours of December 14, Jeff Alm, our backup defensive tackle, lost control of the convertible he was driving. His best friend was thrown from the car and killed. When Jeff saw his friend's body, he was apparently so distraught that he pulled out a gun he had in the car and shot himself.

For the most part, NFL players feel taken care of and safe inside the cocoon teams weave around them. We're so focused on what we do that we're insulated from the problems of others in the outside world. Jeff's shocking death reminded me how fragile our football world and life really are. People will always be more important than wins and losses.

Even so, we had more games to play. Somehow we kept winning. We beat the Steelers and 49ers to run our streak to ten, and were up on the Jets, 14–0, in our regular-season finale when the next blow arrived—literally. Our defensive coordinator, Buddy Ryan, had been feuding all season with offensive coordinator Kevin Gilbride. Ryan apparently felt that the Run and Shoot, with its emphasis on passing, made it difficult to run down the clock and put too much of a strain on the defense. After Kevin called a pass play just before halftime, he and Ryan got into a shouting match. It ended with Ryan punching Kevin on national television.

You can't have animosity between coaches, which fosters animosity between players, and expect to succeed. Despite all our talent, experience, and victories, our team was dysfunctional. Jesus once said, "But everyone who hears these words of mine and does not put them into practice is like a foolish man who built his house on sand. The rain came down, the streams rose, and the winds blew and beat against that house, and it fell with a great crash" (Matthew 7:26–27). That was the Oilers in 1993—we had no solid foundation and were headed for a crash.

We finished the regular season with an eleven-game win streak and a 12–4 record, capturing the AFC Central Division title. For the first time in my career, we'd earned an extra week to rest and prepare for the playoffs. Our opponent the following week was the Kansas City Chiefs, led by Joe Montana, then in the twilight of his great career. We'd blanked the Chiefs, 30–0, earlier that season and led them 10–0 at the half and 13–7 with nine and a half minutes left in the game. The rest of the final quarter, however, was all too familiar. The Chiefs drove seventy-one yards for a touchdown. We lost a fumble on our first play after the kickoff and the Chiefs soon had another touchdown. We were down, 21–13.

As always, we rallied. Warren drove us eighty yards and threw a touchdown pass to Givins, bringing us within a point. But my old Trojan teammate, Marcus Allen, cemented our fate with a twenty-one-yard touchdown burst up the middle. Kansas City beat us, 28–20, ending our season and an era.

We'd qualified for the playoffs seven consecutive seasons, best in the NFL at the time, but never made it to the conference finals. We'd run out of chances. Munch retired. Warren was traded to the Vikings. Buddy Ryan left to become the coach of the Arizona Cardinals. Other veterans were let go. The glory years in Houston were over.

There's nothing quite like the amazing thrills and devastating letdowns of life in the NFL. You're treated like a king one minute, with thousands of people cheering and adoring you, and feel like the lowest bum in the universe the next when you or your teammates make a mistake and things go south. During those playoff years in Houston, I had plenty of opportunities to experience both sensations.

But I was fortunate. I had a growing family—and a growing

faith—to provide perspective. Just eleven days after that crushing loss to the Chiefs, Carrie delivered our fifth child, Michael Caleb (Mikey) Matthews. We named him after Munch. After I saw Mikey, all I wanted was to be with him and my family. We brought him home on a Sunday and I left the next day for the Pro Bowl. I remember how badly I wanted to stay home.

If I learned anything during those up-and-down years in Houston, it was that I wouldn't find lasting contentment in winning games, advancing in the playoffs, or going to Pro Bowls. I loved the game and the victories, but I came to understand that it really was just a game. My family meant so much more to me. My faith, meanwhile, was my foundation. Football victories and awards were more like the sand that Jesus talked about—the rains, floodwaters, and winds of life could wash those accomplishments away and leave me feeling empty. My "house" was built on my relationship with Christ. That was where my value as a person rested. He was, and is, the source of my fulfillment and contentment.

Those truths didn't sink in overnight. I spent a lot of years praying, reading my Bible, and talking with fellow believers—as well as enduring those painful playoff losses—before they resonated in my soul. I would need more reminders in the years to come. Yet I'm thankful to the Lord every day for giving me His perspective and showing me His plan and my purpose in it. His presence gets me through the defeats and makes the delights so much sweeter.

13

OUR KIDS ARE WATCHING

Follow my example, as I follow the example of Christ.

1 Corinthians 11:1

IT SEEMED ONLY A MOMENT THAT I'd taken my eyes off them.

We'd come home from church and Carrie had asked me to watch the kids while she changed clothes. This was in California, back when we had just the three children: Steven was probably four years old, Kevin two, and Marilyn, one. I took them into the backyard. I just wanted a minute to relax and check out the crossword puzzle in the newspaper. The kids couldn't get in trouble in that short a time, right?

A little bit later, Carrie came into the backyard and saw me and Marilyn. "Where are the boys?" she asked.

"They're playing," I said.

"Well, where are they playing?"

"Uh, I don't know. Somewhere in the backyard."

Carrie searched the backyard and couldn't find them. Starting to panic, she ran into the front, then into the street. Suddenly she heard the sound of screeching tires. Down the road, a man leaped out of his car, then began jumping up and down, yelling something and pointing. Carrie turned to look where he'd pointed—at the steeply pitched roof of our two-story house. She was just in time to see, to her horror, the backs of Steven and Kevin as they ran over the peak of the roof and out of sight.

They're dead, Carrie thought. She screamed.

By this time I was searching the backyard myself. When I heard my wife scream, I looked up and spotted the boys running on the roof. "Boys, don't move!" I shouted. Of course they ignored me. I ran back and forth below them, arms out, ready to catch either one if he fell.

Carrie rushed back into the backyard. She saw Marilyn at a locked gate that blocked access to a spiral staircase leading up to our second-floor balcony. The boys had created a makeshift ladder, scaled the gate, gone up the staircase, and climbed from the balcony to the roof. Marilyn was at the bottom of the gate, making a running start and trying futilely to swing her tiny leg over the gate, so that she could join them.

Carrie scooped up Marilyn and hurried to join me. When she arrived and took my place, I hurdled the gate, ran up the staircase to the balcony, scrambled onto the roof, and grabbed Steven and Kevin. It wouldn't be the last time we would need to remove our children from our roof—it happened again after we moved to Texas. Apparently a thirst for adventure—and a desire to scare the daylights out of their parents—is another part of the Matthews DNA. Though the fire marshal wouldn't recommend it, we finally had to screw our windows shut.

I have to admit, I may not have been watching my kids as closely as I should have that morning. If you're a parent, maybe you can relate. But you can be sure that your kids are closely watching and listening to you. For better and worse, dads and moms have tremendous influence on our children.

If I didn't remember this already, I was reminded nearly every time I played a game with my kids. After a big yardage gain against me in our video football game, Steven would taunt me with, "You can't go broke taking a profit!" When Kevin felt inspired to challenge me in hoops, he might say, "Hey, you want a piece of the champ?"

I cringed every time I heard those words. My kids were using the same lines against me that I used on them. Clearly, they'd been listening to my trash talk.

I might not have been thrilled that they were copying my vocabulary, but it was encouraging to Carrie and me to realize that the kids had to be absorbing our positive parenting efforts as well. That was especially important to us when it came to our faith. I wanted them to remember our Sunday mornings in church and our prayers before meals, before bedtime, whenever we had an issue we needed to talk to the Lord about, and before school. On those mornings when I dropped the kids off, I'd repeat something I once heard on the radio: "Have a good and godly day, for of what lasting value is a good day if it's not a godly day as well?" They do remember and still repeat that line today.

I had grand visions of passing on important lessons in theology to our children during family Bible studies. It didn't usually work out that way. We'd get together after dinner in the family room and might start off fine. But then one of the boys or Marilyn would make a funny face and they'd all start giggling. We had trouble staying on task.

One of my lessons involved toothpaste. I handed each of our five kids a small tube and then waved a hundred-dollar bill. "If any of you squeeze the toothpaste out of your tube and can put it back in," I said, "I'll give you this hundred dollars." The message was about hurtful words, that once you say them, you can't take them back.

The kids tried to win that hundred. Once they figured out that their toothpaste wasn't going back into the tube, they got mad. I'm sure they remember that. Whether they recall the lesson is debatable, but at least we were trying.

Carrie and I tried to be good examples in other ways. I took Marilyn on "dates" while Carrie did the same with the boys. It was a way to spend one-on-one time with the kids and make them feel special. We have lots of good memories from those outings.

There were times when our words made an impression. Carrie once heard Steven and Kevin teasing Marilyn, calling her stupid. Marilyn was about seven years old and nearly in tears. Carrie talked to me about it. Then we brought in the boys. "I know you're just teasing your sister," Carrie said, "but when you say those unkind words it makes her feel like you don't love her." Carrie asked the boys to tell Marilyn something they really liked about her and say "I love you." Then we brought Marilyn into the room—she had the saddest look on her face. The boys did as instructed and gave her a hug. Marilyn's frown turned into a grin.

What's great today is that the kids still remember that moment. All of our kids still say "I love you" to each other and still give each other hugs. Apparently Carrie and I got a few things right.

Love is the strongest bond in our family. We're very "family first"—we lean on each other for support. We all like each other and want to hang out together. It's hard for other people to break into that circle, but that's just because we love each other so much.

MARILYN MATTHEWS

When my example was less than perfect, I tried to teach with my words. Though I didn't apply myself as well as I could have as a student, I encouraged our kids to do their best in the classroom. "God has given us these gifts," I told them. "We need to use them. We should strive for excellence in every area of our lives—athletics, academics, our roles as spouses, parents, sons, or daughters."

In many ways, my kids have done a better job than I did in pursuing all-around excellence. I give them a lot of credit for that. I know it's a parent's actions that speak loudest to his kids, not his words. My dad was that example for me and though I sometimes fall short, I've tried to be that kind of father for my children.

In 1994, setting a good example on the field was still a work in progress. I'm not talking about my performance—I'd been to the Pro Bowl each of the previous six years—but those too-frequent occasions when I allowed my intensity to go too far.

One of those occasions was in a preseason game the year before against the Seahawks. I was battling Michael McCrary, a rookie defensive end from Wake Forest. I had a 150-pound advantage on this kid and I was leaning on him hard, but to his credit, he kept coming back for more and never said a word. It started to get on my nerves, to the point that during one play when he turned to run up the field, I cut him in the back of the knees.

It was a foolish, dangerous thing to do. After I calmed down, I couldn't believe I'd done it. I apologized to him after the game. In fact, even after McCrary joined the Ravens and I played against him twice a year, I apologized every time I saw him. "Shut up," he'd say. "Don't worry about it." It got to be a joke between us.

My behavior wasn't a joke, however. I realized I had too much of that going on—retaliations, unnecessary fights, cursing at referees. I knew that God wanted me to play hard, to always do my best. But to represent Him well, I needed to eliminate the other stuff. In my efforts to be more like Christ, I still had a long way to go.

The 1994 Oilers also had a long way to go. The uniforms were still Columbia blue and white and the helmets still featured an oil derrick, but we were a very different team than the one fans had cheered for the year before. With Warren Moon traded, our new quarterback was Cody Carlson, a great guy and a regular at our team Bible studies. Cody's tenure as starter lasted for two-and-a-half quarters, as he was sidelined by a knee injury in our opening-game loss to the Colts. It was a sign of things to come.

We managed to beat the Bengals in week four, 20–13, but that was one of the few highlights from that season. We kept losing games by three points—to the Cowboys, the Browns, the Raiders, and then the Steelers in overtime, 12–9. I had to admit that our defense was outperforming our offense. We struggled to score.

With our record at 1–9, Bud Adams dismissed both Jack Pardee and Kevin Gilbride. Our new head coach was our defensive coordinator and one of my old teammates at USC, Jeff Fisher.

Jeff and I played together for two years in college, though I didn't know him well. We actually had several connections. His wife, Julie, was from Arcadia High School, two classes ahead of me. I also used to catch for Julie's younger brother when he pitched and we played in Pony League. Jeff had been coaching in the NFL for ten years and had done a great job as our defensive coordinator. I was excited when he took over. I knew he was a quality guy with a team-first attitude, which we needed. The fact that he was from USC was frosting on the cake.

We still lost the next five games, including three more close ones. But we knocked off the Jets in our season finale, 24–10, to give us some optimism going into the off-season.

We finished the year 2–14. Our ten-game drop-off was the largest from one season to the next in the history of the NFL. What's funny is that despite our miserable record, I actually enjoyed that season more than the one before. All the strange events of 1993 had taken a mental and emotional toll. We may not have had as much talent, but we were back to just playing football. That felt right to me. Though the fans may not have agreed, I believed that it was a step in the right direction.

I wouldn't be surprised if a few die-hard Houston fans were tempted to hit the bottle after our descent into the AFC Central Division cellar. As for me, though, that season didn't change my drinking habits. I already had an established routine.

My attitude about drinking alcohol in those days was that it was just part of the NFL culture. From my first training camp, when my new teammates gathered in the evening around that fridge in the dorms, I'd seen that hoisting a few cold ones was the preferred method for unwinding from the pressures of being a professional football player. It also seemed to help build team spirit and trust between us. I still have fond memories of Earl Campbell sitting there singing Merle Haggard and Willie Nelson tunes. I wanted to fit in and I wasn't a problem drinker. At the time, it wasn't a big issue to me.

My parents came from the era of cocktail parties, so it wasn't strange to see them with a drink in their hands. But Bruz didn't drink and I wanted to be like him, so I never had a sip of alcohol growing up. I drank only a handful of times while in college. It wasn't until I reached the NFL that I made it a regular practice. During the season, Thursday was our camaraderie night. Munch and I and some of the other guys would go to Jackie's Ice House, a place near the Astrodome. And we always went out and had a few beers after games.

My competitive nature didn't help matters. Being a Matthews, I wanted to be the best at everything. That of course included drinking. A few times, it led me to do dumb things I never would have done if I had been completely sober.

One of those things occurred on the way to training camp one year. Munch, Dean Steinkuhler, and I were in Munch's Eddie Bauer Bronco, driving on Interstate 10 between Houston and San Antonio. As happens when one has too much to drink—and seemed to happen especially often to Dean—we reached a point where we needed to relieve ourselves. Instead of stopping at a rest stop, gas station, or restaurant, however, we chose to do our business behind a billboard that featured Noah's Ark (I think it was an advertisement for a petting zoo).

Actually, only Munch and Dean emptied their bladders behind the sign. When they returned to the front of the billboard, they were a man short. "Where's Bruce?" Munch said. That's when they heard what sounded like rainwater splattering on the ground. I'd climbed to the top of the billboard and was now relieving myself along the starboard side of the ark. Not exactly an entry for my résumé.

I rationalized my drinking. I told myself I could handle it. But I know there were times I drove home when I shouldn't have been driving. I didn't have as much control over my drinking as I pretended to have.

In 1995 I was relaxing with our family and friends on our property in Sugar Land, a suburb of Houston. We'd recently purchased fifty-one acres of mostly pastureland, and planned to build Carrie's dream home there. One of my favorite evening activities was to cut down a few trees, build a roaring fire, cook hot dogs, and bask in the warmth while downing a beer or two.

Steven was ten years old then. On one of those nights on our property, he was sitting on a cooler filled with beer. "Hey Steven," one of my friends said, "why don't you get me and your dad a beer?"

As soon as I heard those words, I frowned. I don't want my kids bringing me beer. "Never mind, Steven," I said. "I'll get 'em."

I thought often about that moment over the following months. It bothered me. I had seen people close to me struggle with drinking. It had changed their behavior and even led to ugly incidents. I could warn my children about the dangers of alcohol, but I realized my actions would mean more than my words. They were watching me. Carrie didn't drink, but I did. Did I want my kids drinking because they saw Dad do it?

There's a Bible passage that reads, "Let us therefore make every effort to do what leads to peace and to mutual edification . . . It is better not to eat meat or drink wine or to do anything else that will cause your brother or sister to fall" (Romans 14:19, 21). My kids would eventually decide for themselves whether or not they would drink alcohol. But I didn't want to make that choice for them by encouraging them to drink before they were ready to choose.

Two years later I was still weighing the issue. During training camp, on a morning when I'd been out drinking the night before, I got onto the elevator at our practice facility. A rookie free agent got onto the elevator with me. He told me he'd just been released. Then he shook my hand.

"I just want to tell you what an honor it's been to be here in camp with you and be in the Bible study with you," he said. "You've set a great example and I really respect you for that."

His words were like a blow to the gut. I hoped he couldn't smell my breath because it probably still had an odor of beer.

What am I doing? I thought. *Is this what I'm about? Am I bringing glory to the Lord with my drinking? What kind of message am I sending to my teammates?* The truth was that I didn't even like the taste of beer. The only reason I drank was to get that feel-good buzz. But what was the cost?

It took me a while to work through that mental battle and make a decision. But once I made up my mind, that was it. *I'm not going to miss waking up with a headache,* I thought. *I don't need alcohol.* More important, I'm not going to influence my kids to stumble because of this.

I stopped drinking on May 2, 1998. Other than one glass of

champagne, I haven't had a drop since. I know there are lots of opinions on this particular issue, but for me it was the right choice.

Today, nearly all of my kids are out of the house and living on their own. I don't have the opportunity to guide and shape them on a daily basis like I once did. But I know they're still watching me. I just pray that they'll overlook my imperfections, remember the good examples and lessons, and continue to grow closer to God and the plan He has for each of their lives. As a father, I couldn't ask for anything more.

My dad, Clay Sr., playing football at Georgia Tech in the late 1940s

Clay Sr. playing his guitar with some teammates in the early 1950s

Nine years old, first year of Little League baseball (1971)

Pool games with the Matthews brothers (1972)

TOP: With my mom, Daisy, on Photo Day at USC in 1979, just before my first season

LEFT: First year of basketball at ten years old (1972)

LEFT: Carrie and me at the Stars and Crescent Ball (1980)

BELOW: Our wedding day, May 28, 1983

The Matthews Bowl in December 1983, the first and last time Daisy saw Clay and me compete against each other

Me with Steven (1985)

Kevin, me, and Steven on Halloween night. I reported for the season four days later, ending my holdout (1987)

Me with kids (Marilyn, Kevin, and Steven) when there were only three (1989)

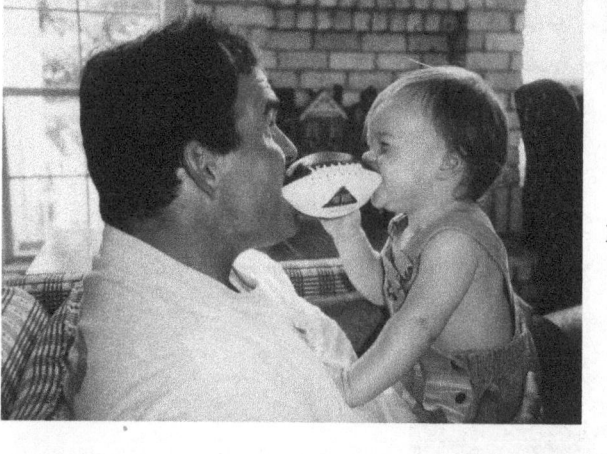

Mikey and me (1995)

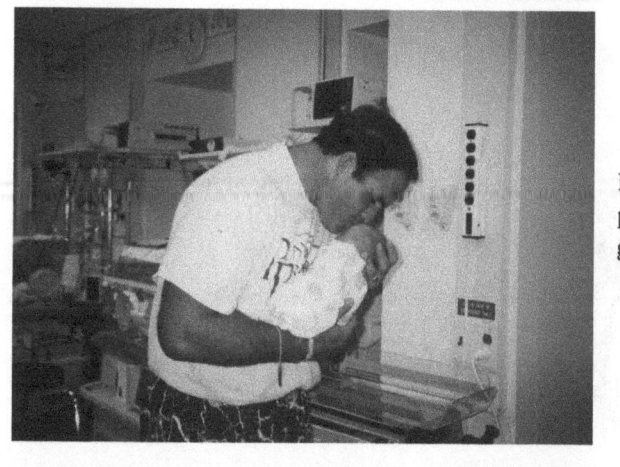

Here I am giving little preemie Luke his first kiss good night (1999)

With Mikey during my first year coaching youth football (2002)

With Titans owner Bud Adams
when the Titans retired my jersey
(2002) *Photo courtesy of Donn Jones,
Tennessee Titans*

Gwenie and me on an afternoon
bike ride (2005)

With Dad at the Titans
game, where I was pre-
sented with the Hall of
Fame ring (2007)

The Matthews family at the Hall of Fame ceremony (2007)

Mike Munchak, Kevin, and me with the Titans (2009)

From left to right: Me, Kevin, Clay III, and Clay Junior at a Packers/Titans game (2012) *Photo courtesy of Donn Jones, Tennessee Titans*

Entire family after an Aggie game (2014)

Here I am with Jake after he was selected in the first round by the Atlanta Falcons (2014)

With my two grandsons, Sawyer and Weston, in South Carolina's Isle of Palms (2015)

14

IN ALL THINGS

Trust in the Lord with all your heart
and lean not on your own understanding.

PROVERBS 3:5

MY CONTRACT EXPIRED AGAIN AFTER THE 1994 season. Thanks to the recent collective bargaining agreement, I was truly a free agent for the first time—I could sign with any team. A few other teams had expressed interest, but I wanted to stay with the Oilers. We'd just purchased that property and planned to build a house. We had five kids and wanted them to go full-time in one school system. I loved the Oilers fans and the people of Houston had always treated me well.

In addition, Munch had joined the Oilers coaching staff after retiring and had been retained by Jeff Fisher. They and the other coaches were good people who I was sure would point our team in the right direction. As far as I was concerned, Houston was where I belonged.

By this time, I'd personally taken over my contract negotiations. I told the organization, "Look, I'm not going to play games. I have no desire to play for a team anywhere else. I want to be here."

"Fine," I was told. "Let us finish our other free agent contracts, then we'll take care of you." Though I missed a few days of training camp and the first preseason game, we quickly settled on terms. In early August—I believe it was the eighth, my birthday—I signed a four-year deal. I was thirty-four years old and ready to put down our family's roots. Considering some of the contentious negotiations I'd had in the past, I thought everything had worked out great.

Three days later, I was with the Oilers in Knoxville, Tennessee, for a scheduled preseason game with the Washington Redskins. Surprisingly, our owner was there too. The team was assembled at our hotel so Mr. Adams could address us. "Hey," he said, "I just want to tell you guys that we've struck a deal to move the team to Nashville."

My jaw almost hit the floor. *Nashville? Are you kidding me? You guys knew about this three days ago and didn't tell me?* I was furious.

I was aware of Mr. Adams' frustrations with the Oilers' Astrodome lease and his efforts to build a new stadium in Houston, which had made little progress. But I had no idea that he was considering moving the team. If I'd known about the prospective move, I certainly would have explored options with other teams. I don't know that I would have left the Oilers because I did have faith in the coaching staff. But I couldn't believe that the front-office people knew I wanted to be in Houston, knew about the move, and let me sign a contract anyway. I felt betrayed.

As I've said, I'm a guy who appreciates his routine. I don't even like having my weekend plans rearranged, let alone a change in where

I want to live for the next four years. I was frustrated that the future Carrie and I had decided on had been ripped away from us.

I was even unhappy with the Lord. "I had a pretty good plan," I told Him. "What was the matter with it?" Though I'd matured in my faith since my brief holdout before my rookie season and the much longer one in 1987, I sometimes still forget to look at situations from God's perspective.

There's a verse in the Bible that says, "Count it pure joy, my brothers, whenever you face trials of many kinds, because you know that the testing of your faith develops perseverance" (James 1:2). That's how God works—He allows us to experience problems and the unsettledness that comes with unexpected changes so that we will learn to lean on Him, trust Him more, expand our faith, and grow in our character. Yes, trials are inconvenient, uncomfortable, even painful. Yet He promises to go through them with us.

I had my own life plans in 1995 and they did not include a move to Nashville. But neither God nor Bud Adams had consulted me. I was going to have to live with it.

The transition to Tennessee wasn't actually scheduled to happen until the 1998 season. Nashville voters had to first approve funds for a new stadium. I crossed my fingers and hoped that the proposed move would fall through.

Everything about the preseason that year seemed out of whack. First I missed the opening of camp because of my contract negotiations. Then came the announcement about the Nashville move. Then our third preseason game in the Dome against the Chargers was canceled because the grounds crew couldn't get a newly installed piece of Astroturf to mesh with the old turf. The game was delayed for two hours before the announcement was made, which was met with a chorus of boos. Finally, in our last preseason game, we got shut out by the Cowboys, 10–0. Not an auspicious start.

When the regular season began, many Houston fans stayed home. After the disappointments of previous years, our performance the year before, and ownership's announced intention to leave the city, a lot of people were either angry or had lost interest. I couldn't blame them. Compared to the raucous old days, the Astrodome now felt like a library.

Yet our product on the field was improving. We'd signed Mark Stepnoski, formerly a Pro Bowl center for the Cowboys. At six foot two and 260 pounds, Mark was undersized for a lineman, yet he excelled because his technique was so sound. Because of Mark's addition, I moved from center to Munch's old spot, the only position I'd yet to play on the offensive line: left guard. We had a new quarterback, Chris Chandler, and our defense remained strong. We also had a rookie quarterback with an impressive arm and the ability to run. Steve McNair would need time to adjust to the NFL, but I could tell he had potential. He became the toughest quarterback I ever played with. We won seven games in 1995.

We drafted another important addition in 1996, Ohio State running back and Heisman Trophy winner Eddie George. He was a fitness freak, an amazing physical specimen at six foot three and 235 pounds, and had a great attitude. I loved playing with Eddie. In his first season with us, he gained 1,368 yards rushing and was named the NFL's Rookie of the Year.

I remained at left guard that season and continued to contribute on special teams. I'd had a few proud moments on special teams over the years. A punt coverage play in 1986 was one of my career high-lights. We were playing the Steelers in the Dome and punting to Pro Bowl return man Louis Lipps. I sprinted downfield after the punt was away and noticed no other blue shirts around me. As I got closer to Lipps, I saw two Steelers sprinting at me, one on each side. All right, I thought. *I'm just going to keep running, brace for the hit, and hope it's not too ugly.*

The pair of Steelers did indeed hit me—at the same instant. Some-how, the momentum of one canceled the momentum of the other. They bounced off me and I was still running—I didn't even break stride. Lipps caught the ball and I made an unassisted, open-field tackle. None of my offensive line buddies were watching at the time, of course. But when we all sat down to view the play on film the next week, they whooped and hollered as if they'd done it themselves. It was a great moment.

On Thanksgiving Day in 1992 I made another unassisted tackle on a punt to Mel Gray, the Lions' All-Pro kick returner. You could count the tackles I made in my career on one hand, so each time was a thrill.

I was less thrilled, however, about another special teams play in that 1996 season. Field goal protection is one of the most thankless jobs in the NFL—it's highly stressful and you only get noticed if your man breaks through the line. I'd never had anyone get through me to block a field goal before and no one did it to me since, but the ex-ception was in a game against Pittsburgh. We were down 10–0 in the first quarter when I lined up to snap for a forty-seven-yard field goal attempt. Joel Steed, a three-hundred-pound bull of a nose tackle, was across from me.

When blocking for a field goal, I usually put out both hands and hooked guys in the crook of my arm. That's what I tried to do this time. But I found myself facing a perfect storm of leverage and timing. All of a sudden my body was flying in the air. It was like being at the beach when a wave catches you and you realize there's nothing you can do. I was thrown to the ground and thought, *Man, why am I looking up at blue sky?* In the next instant, I heard a sickening double-thud—the first being the sound of Al Del Greco's foot kicking the ball, and the second being Steeler defensive end Brentson Buckner blocking it.

We lost that game but still managed to improve our record from the year before, finishing 8–8. Still feeling rejected, many of our old fans were unimpressed. Our opponents often had more rooters in the Astrodome than we did. Our team was progressing—and so were the organization's moving plans. Nashville's voters said yes to a referendum on a new stadium. Then in spring 1997, the Oilers worked out a deal to get out of their stadium lease a year early. Like it or not, I was headed to Tennessee.

I was about to turn thirty-six. After fourteen years in the league, I wondered if I'd hang up my cleats if I didn't enjoy playing in Nashville. Since I'd been hoping the move would somehow fall apart, I hadn't made any plans for the family. We'd just had the foundation laid for our new house. Carrie and I decided she and the kids would stay in Houston for the season and come up for home games while I rented an apartment in Nashville.

Our new name was the Tennessee Oilers. Since we didn't have a stadium yet, we played our home games three hours west of Nashville in Liberty Bowl Memorial Stadium, the home field of the University of Memphis Tigers. Team officials had often promised that everything would be great when we got to Tennessee, but most people in Memphis weren't excited about supporting Nashville's team. We had only seventeen thousand in the stands for a game against the Bengals. We didn't draw any more fans than we had those last couple years in Houston.

One big plus that made the move easier for me to handle was Munch. My best friend was now my coach—he'd been promoted and was responsible for the offensive line and tight ends. It's not that he took it easy on me. If anything, I felt more pressure than ever to perform well. But we spent a lot of hours talking about how to play on the line. I realized I'd often gotten by on athleticism and wasn't as fundamentally sound as I could have been. Munch explained technique in a way that made sense to me. At thirty-six, I didn't have the same strength and stamina I'd had at twenty-six. But my technique improved so much that I began playing better than ever.

What wasn't better than ever was living alone. I had nothing to do at my apartment but read, watch television, and play video games. I'm not much of a cook—my supposed "dinner" on too many nights was a few bowls of Frosted Mini-Wheats. I felt so sorry for myself that a couple of times I downed some beers to try to get rid of my blues. Then I thought about what I was doing. *Are you kidding me? Are you drinking alone now?* It was another turning point that led me to give up alcohol the next year.

I missed my family tremendously. I spent a lot of time that year with Munch and the other coaches, hanging around their offices and eating meals with them. I also visited the Munchaks' house often. But I couldn't wait for our home games and the chance to see Carrie and the kids. On those weekends, they would fly up from Houston to Nashville on Friday night. Then, on Sunday, they got up at dawn to catch the three-hour bus trip to Memphis, watched the game, and then bused back to Nashville. They'd spend Sunday night with me at the apartment and fly home the next day. We didn't usually do anything special. It was just great to have them around.

I hated being apart from them. On one of those Fridays when we'd planned for everyone to fly up, Carrie called: Kevin had jumped down from the top of a jungle gym and broken both ankles. They wouldn't be coming until Saturday. Hearing about Kevin and knowing I'd have to wait those extra hours to see everyone was devastating.

As hard as it was to be separated from my family, I realize in hindsight that my time alone in Nashville was a blessing. I began to understand more than ever how important each of them was to me. Though I talked to Carrie every night on the phone, I missed her presence. I also missed all the noise and turmoil—even the fights—that the kids created. I wanted to be there to help them with homework and hear about their day. I felt I'd sometimes taken Carrie and the kids for granted. Now they were managing life for the most part without me. My admiration for Carrie's ability to parent five kids soared even higher. That time in Nashville gave me a new and deep sense of gratitude and appreciation for my family.

The time alone was a blessing in another way—it allowed me to focus more on developing my faith. Back in Houston, Oilers chaplain Greg Headington had moved on and been replaced by Mike Myers, a gung-ho former high school coach who was affiliated with the Fellowship for Christian Athletes. Mike challenged me to be more than a casual Christian. My faith definitely grew during the Bible studies and chapel services he led.

We had a new chaplain when we moved to Tennessee: James "Mitch" Mitchell, a country boy from Mississippi. Mitch was the perfect guy for me to get to know at that point in my life. Since I had the time, we went out for dinner often and talked from thirty to ninety minutes nearly every night. I had a lot on my mind spiritually, including what obedience to God meant and my concerns about my drinking. As we talked, I realized I didn't want to straddle the fence with my faith. Jesus said that was worse than having no faith: "I know your deeds, that you are neither cold nor hot. I wish you were either one or the other! So, because you are lukewarm—neither hot nor cold—I am about to spit you out of my mouth" (Revelation 3:15–16). I needed to be all in.

Mitch was a good friend and mentor when I needed one. Two years later, Reggie Pleasant became the team chaplain. All four of the NFL chaplains I got to know were outstanding guys and friends who encouraged me so much spiritually. I hate to think where I'd be without their influence.

For me today, faith often comes down to trusting that God has my best interests at heart. I like to be in control, and I've spent too many hours whining about what I don't have instead of remembering what I do have. But I'm learning that everything works better when I stop trying to get my way and manage every detail and just allow Him to be in charge. When I face problems, I've gotten better at saying, "Lord, I don't really want to go through this, but I know You've got a plan. You've been good to me for the first fifty-plus years of my life. I'm going to trust You with the rest of it."

That trust came a little bit easier in 1998. The Oilers were on the move again, at least in terms of our home field. Because of the lack of support in Memphis, our new base was Vanderbilt Stadium in Nashville. We equaled our record from the season before, again going 8–8. But it was a much more enjoyable year, since Carrie and the kids now lived with me in Nashville. I'd survived my season away from the family and became a wiser person because of it.

The Bible says, "And we know that in all things God works for the good of those who love him, who have been called according to his purpose" (Romans 8:28). That was definitely the case in my move to Nashville. When I stop to think about it, I realize that's always been the case.

15

MUSIC CITY MIRACLES

Focus on the journey, not the destination.
Joy is found not in finishing an activity but in doing it.
GREG ANDERSON

I WAS TOO HEAVY.

Every offensive lineman wants bulk, of course. It helps to have a big body when you're trying to slow down those behemoths on defense. But I'd played 1998 at 315 pounds, which felt like too much to me. I thought that if I dropped some weight, I'd be quicker off the snap. So I lost fifteen pounds during the offseason.

Now that the team was finally moving into our permanent Nashville home, Adelphia Coliseum, the organization had decided to retire the Oilers name. We'd been rechristened the Tennessee Titans. I thought that the new me looked sleeker in our new navy blue and white uniforms. I figured when you look good, you feel good and you play better.

My weight and our uniforms weren't all that changed: We had a new attitude to match. Les Steckel, our offensive coordinator, believed that if something worked for us, we should just stay with it. We'd already had success wearing down opponents with Eddie George running the ball. Eddie had gained well over a thousand rushing yards in each of his first three years and been named to the Pro Bowl the last two. But in our second preseason game, Les took that mindset to a new level.

We were playing the Arizona Cardinals at Sun Devil Stadium in Tempe. Even though it was evening, the temperature was still about a hundred degrees. We were dying on the field, the sweat pouring off us. In the middle of a long drive, Les called Fifteen Bob, a weak-side zone run that meant Eddie would read the defense and choose a hole somewhere between the tackles. He made a nice gain. Les called the exact same play again.

And again.

And again.

Les was making a point, both to the Cardinals and to us. This was our identity. He didn't care if the other team knew what was coming. We were going to impose our will on other teams. The only problem was that we all felt ready to collapse from heat exhaustion.

In the huddle after the fourth Fifteen Bob, Steve McNair had his hands over the earholes in his helmet so he could hear the next play being radioed in from Les. At the same time, Eddie, breathing hard, said to Steve, "Dude . . . throw it . . . do something else. I can't run another one." I thought, if he calls that play again, I'm going to keel over out here.

While waiting for the next play call, Eddie raised his head and locked eyes with mine. The look on his face said, *He wouldn't . . . would he?*

An instant later, Steve announced the next play: "Far right. Fifteen Bob."

Today, whenever I see Eddie, I remind him of that moment in the huddle and we both shake our heads and laugh. It wasn't so funny then, but Les had set the tone for the type of team we'd be that year. We weren't going to outfox our opponents. We would do what we did best and challenge them to stop us.

That approach seemed to work at the beginning of our season opener in Nashville. In front of sixty-five thousand brand-new NFL fans, we scored three touchdowns, kicked a field goal, and recorded a safety in the first quarter and a half to lead Cincinnati, 26–7. The crowd was into it. The Bengals weren't going to be pushovers, however. They stormed back to take a 35–26 advantage with eight minutes left in the game.

Maybe I'd become a fatalist after seeing us blow too many close ones in the past. I couldn't believe we were going to lose our opening game.

But we didn't. Steve hit Eddie with a seventeen-yard touchdown pass, our defense held, and we moved efficiently down the field as time ran down. With eight seconds left, I snapped the ball and Al Del Greco booted a thirty-three-yard field goal to give us a 36–35 victory.

If every game was going to be like this, Titans fans would get their money's worth.

The bad news that followed our victory was that Steve McNair had an inflamed disc and needed surgery. In fact, his back surgeon was the same as mine. Steve would miss the next five games. Yet, behind his replacement, veteran Neil O'Donnell, we kept rolling. Our week three opponent, the Jacksonville Jaguars, had won our division the year before and led 17–7 going into the fourth quarter. But we came back with two field goals and a touchdown to win 20–19.

After four years at left guard, the coaches had moved me back to center for the first few games of 1999. For week five against the Baltimore Ravens, they returned me to left guard, where I stayed for the rest of the season. The Ravens had a tremendous defense that included Tony Siragusa, Rob Burnett, and my old friend Michael McCrary on the line, Ray Lewis and Peter Boulware at linebacker, and Rod Woodson at free safety. The next year, they added Sam Adams at defensive tackle to make one of the great defenses in NFL history. Every game against them felt like an epic struggle, but we prevailed in this one, 14–11.

We went into our bye week with a 5–1 record, ready for some well-deserved relaxation. It didn't quite turn out that way for the Matthews family, however.

Carrie was pregnant again and due in December. On Saturday morning of our bye weekend, she went into premature labor. I took Carrie to the hospital but the staff sent us back home, saying it was too early to be in labor. She continued to have contractions during the day. After we'd gone to bed that night, she woke up, her contractions more intense than ever. She called her doctor to say she'd reached the final stage of labor, but like the hospital staff, the doctor said it was too early and that Carrie was too calm to be in labor, and that she should go back to bed.

Carrie hung up and woke me up. "I'm having this baby," she said. "You've got to get me to the hospital."

When we arrived, the staff tried to turn Carrie away yet again, once more saying she was too calm. "What do you want me to do, yell and scream?" Carrie said. "It's my sixth child." She walked past the staff members and headed for the maternity ward. When a nurse caught up, she said, "Ma'am, what are you doing?"

"I'm having a baby," Carrie said. "It's coming out now." A nurse finally took a look, then slammed an emergency button.

Luke Jackson Matthews was born within minutes. (My admiration for Confederate general Stonewall Jackson inspired the middle name.) Luke was six pounds, one-and-a-half ounces, huge for a baby born six-and-a-half-weeks early but completely healthy. I'd wondered what I would do if our baby was born on a Sunday. Would I miss the game? The last thing I wanted was to create another "Babygate." Since it was our bye week, however, it worked out perfectly. It had started to feel like we were getting an extra measure of blessings that year.

● ● ●

The hype was heavy for our week-eight game against the unbeaten St. Louis Rams and their new quarterback, Kurt Warner. Steve McNair was back after his surgery. Some of the media said the game might be a Super Bowl preview. Our crowd was so loud that the Rams couldn't hear Warner call signals—they were whistled eight times for false start penalties, five of those penalties by right tackle Fred Miller.

Just as in our season opener against Cincinnati, we grabbed a quick lead and then allowed our opponent to come back. We led 21–0 after the first quarter, but when Warner threw a touchdown pass with just over two minutes left, our advantage was only 24–21. Then the Rams recovered their onside kick. They drove to our twenty-yard line, but with twenty seconds left, Jeff Wilkins' thirty-eight-yard field goal attempt was wide right. We'd pulled out another tight victory.

That win definitely built up our confidence. I began to think that this could be a special season. I'd been in the NFL for seventeen years and been part of only two playoff victories. I knew my chances for going deep into the postseason were running out. No Matthews had ever played in the Super Bowl. Maybe this was the year.

Going into Baltimore in week thirteen, our record stood at 9–2. Unfortunately, the Ravens thumped us, 41–14. The only memorable moment from that game occurred after our first offensive play. The officials stopped the clock and someone announced over the stadium loudspeaker that I had just tied the record set by Jackie Slater, the great Rams tackle, for games played by an NFL offensive lineman (259). I ran to the sideline so a referee could present me with the game ball. It was a strange moment since we were in Baltimore and the fans had no love for us Titans. I remember saying, "Do we really have to do this?"

I enjoyed being recognized the next week, however. We hosted the 6–6 Raiders. The NFL flew in Slater, who presented me with a commemorative football at midfield before the game. Since I'd spent so many years growing up in the Los Angeles area, I was very aware of Jackie's success with the Rams when they played there. It was an honor to share that moment with him.

I felt honored in a different way when I posed for a group of photographers. One of them said, "Hey Matthews, smile!" I suddenly realized who it was—my old Arcadia buddy, Dave Samarzich. "What the heck are you doing out here?" I said.

Sam had dabbled in photography in high school. Since then, he'd gotten more serious about it and he decided to fly out to record my special day. After that, Sam even started shooting one or two Titans games a season and would talk to me on the sideline. Having him there when I broke the games-played record was a fun surprise. My day was complete when we knocked off the Raiders, 21–14.

We won the last three games of the regular season as well, including a 41–14 thrashing of Jacksonville. Our final record was excellent, 13–3, but the Jaguars still won the division by going 14–2. Their only losses were the two games against us.

It was wild card playoff time again. Our opponent was an old postseason nemesis, the Buffalo Bills. Nearly sixty-seven thousand fans jammed into sold-out Adelphia Coliseum for the first-ever Titans playoff game. The weather was cloudy and a cool forty degrees, the way I liked it. At the start, both offenses were cool as well—neither team scored in the first quarter. In fact, the first points were recorded early in the second quarter when our All-Pro rookie, defensive end Jevon Kearse, sacked Buffalo quarterback Rob Johnson in the end zone for a safety.

We extended our lead to 12–0 at halftime on a McNair touchdown and Del Greco field goal. Sure enough, though, the Bills rallied. A pair of touchdowns, the second followed by a dropped pass on a conversion attempt, gave Buffalo a 13–12 lead with eleven minutes to go in the game. After a punt by each team, we had the ball with just over six minutes left.

Les Steckel had shown us the plan—pound 'em with the ground game—back in that Arizona preseason game and when we needed it most, we stuck to it. After a pair of short passes and a McNair run, we handed the ball to Eddie George five straight times. Every play was either up the middle or off tackle. With two minutes left, we were on Buffalo's sixteen-yard line. Steve lost a couple yards on third down, so it was time for a field goal. I snapped the ball and Al booted it. The kick was wobbly, but it went through. We were up, 15–13.

The Bills would not die. A thirty-three-yard kickoff return put them on their own thirty-nine-yard line. Passing and running out of a shotgun formation, Rob Johnson moved them down the field in a hurry. I watched from the sideline, my frustration mounting.

Are you kidding me? After all we've been through—the lame-duck year in Houston, those tough two years in Tennessee, the way everything's turned around this season—after all that, we're going to lose this one?

From our thirty-two-yard line, Johnson—playing with only one shoe since the other had come off the play before—completed a nine-yard pass to Peerless Price, who was pushed out of bounds. With twenty seconds left, the Bills had a first down on our twenty-three-yard line.

Kicker Steve Christie walked onto the field for a field goal attempt. They could have run more time off the clock, but I'm guessing they wanted to leave time for a second try if something went wrong. Christie's forty-one-yard kick went between the uprights. Buffalo took back the lead, 16–15.

Sixteen seconds left.

Every Saturday, one of the last things we did at practice was run a trick play called Home Run Throwback. It was designed by special-teams coordinator Alan Lowry for kickoff returns. I wasn't involved, so I wasn't that familiar with it. It was a desperation play, made even more desperate this day since the guy who usually practiced it and was supposed to end up with the ball, Derrick Mason, had gotten injured earlier in the game.

Our season depended on this play. Basically, we were as good as dead.

I stood on the sideline, thoroughly disgusted about the situation and powerless to do anything but watch. Christie kicked off, a shorter-than-usual kick caught by Lorenzo Neal on our twenty-four-yard line in the middle of the field. Neal took a couple steps to the right, but he wasn't supposed to have the ball on Home Run Throwback, so he handed it to tight end Frank Wycheck. Frank took a couple more steps to the right. With Bills linebacker Sam Rogers diving at him, Wycheck turned and threw the ball across the field to wide receiver Kevin Dyson with what was supposed to be a lateral.

Dyson was on the Titans' side of the field. On the sideline, I stood only a few feet away when he caught Wycheck's throw. *Huh,* I thought. *I can't believe this has worked so far.*

I looked down field and saw nearly all blue jerseys ahead of Dyson—there were few Bills players in position to tackle him. Dyson sprinted down the sideline. All of a sudden it sank in—he's going to score!

Dyson raced untouched into the end zone and the crowd went crazy.

I wasn't ready to celebrate yet. I thought, *There's got to be a flag.* Though I'd been close to Dyson when he caught Wycheck's toss, I didn't have the angle to know if it had been a lateral or an illegal forward pass. I knew it was close.

The referees knew it too. They huddled for a review on instant replay.

The seconds ticked off. It began to feel like hours. I stood on the field with my helmet on, ready to snap for the extra point and waiting along with everyone else in the stadium in agonizing anticipation. The longer the review went, though, the more hopeful I became. *These guys probably realize an angry mob's going to grab them if they rule against us. It can't go against us.*

Nearly four minutes after the score, referee Phil Luckett walked onto the field and made the announcement: "The play stands. It was a lateral." He raised his hands over his head: "Touchdown." The crowd erupted in a full-throated roar.

It's known as the Music City Miracle. It was amazing.

A minute later, I ran to the locker room, thinking about the heartbreak of the Comeback all those years before. I was the only player left on the team from that nightmare. A film crew recorded me saying, "Man, this is better than the '92 game. Thirty-five to three? Forget it!" All the disgust and disappointment from that loss had finally been washed away. It was an awesome feeling.

Our next opponent was the Indianapolis Colts, led by second-year quarterback Peyton Manning. The first half was a battle of field goals. They led us 9–6 at intermission. But early in the third quarter, Eddie George busted loose on a sixty-eight-yard touchdown run and we held on to win 19–16.

After the game, with all the players gathered around in the locker room, Jeff Fisher addressed us: "Hey, we've got a guy here who's never been this far in the playoffs, who's been here through all the bad years. I want to present him with this game ball." Jeff handed the ball to me and everyone cheered and whistled. I got a little choked up over that one.

The AFC Championship was played in Jacksonville. The Jaguars beat everybody they played that season—except us. Even though they were up on us at halftime, 14–7, I had the sense that we were more confident than they were, that we knew we would win. In the third quarter, we found our groove. After a touchdown and field goal, Josh Evans and Jason Fisk took down Jacksonville quarterback Mark Brunell in the end zone for a safety. On the next play, Derrick Mason ran back the Jaguars' kick eighty yards for a touchdown.

Oh, my gosh, I thought, *we're going to the Super Bowl.* So many times I'd watched other players at this moment and wondered what the feeling would be like. Now, as I looked at Munch and other buddies on the team, I knew. It was great.

The final score was 33–14. We flew back to Nashville that night and met a crowd of more than forty thousand happy fans at Adelphia Coliseum. It turned into a pep rally. I even addressed the crowd, which was out of character for me: "They said when there were sixteen seconds left in the Music City Miracle that we were finished. And we showed 'em!" The crowd roared. "Then they said we couldn't beat that Peyton guy up in Indianapolis. But we took care of business." The crowd erupted again.

"And then they said we couldn't beat the Jaguars three times in one year. Now they're saying we can't beat the Rams in the Super Bowl after we whipped them in week eight? Are you kidding me?"

I was channeling my inner Hulk Hogan. The fans loved it. My only regret was that my family wasn't with me to share the moment—after the Buffalo game, I'd put them all on a flight back to Houston, so the kids could start school there. They'd missed the last two victories.

But there was no doubt they'd be there for the next game. At last, we were going to the big dance.

Super Bowl week was a blur. This was one of the few times when the NFL scheduled only a week between the conference title games and the championship, rather than the usual two weeks. Between the travel to Atlanta, meetings, practices, and media obligations, it wasn't enough.

I do remember a few highlights. During media day, I had the chance to talk about my faith in a handful of interviews. On Thursday, the NFL put on a welcome party for players' families. It was Mikey's sixth birthday, so the band played "Happy Birthday" for him.

There was also the day when I drove a few of my teammates back to our hotel after a meal. I decided we needed to create a little competition, so I made everyone take their shirts off and roll their windows down. The winner would be the one who kept his window down the longest. Atlanta was covered with ice at the time, with temperatures in the teens, so the weather was definitely bracing. Since I was driving, however, I had the advantage of being able to turn on the heat for my part of the car. I believe I won that contest.

The contest I really wanted to win, of course, was the Super Bowl. We were confident going into the game, but in the first half we didn't show what we were capable of. The Rams gained nearly three hundred yards to our eighty-nine. We were fortunate to be down only 9–0.

In the locker room at intermission, Les Steckel reminded us what we were about. "Look, we've been trying to be too cute, too fancy," he said. "We're going to come out running the ball. We're going to pound 'em."

We didn't start out in the second half any better than the first. On our opening drive we had a field goal blocked. Then St. Louis drove to a score on a Warner touchdown pass to Torry Holt. We trailed 16–0.

But then Les's strategy started to pay off. With Steve and Eddie alternating on runs, we ground down the field. Eddie scored on a one-yard rush and the lead was cut to 16–6. In the fourth quarter, we did it again, this time alternating rushes by Eddie with short passes from Steve. Eddie scored another touchdown and we trailed only 16–13.

When our defense held, we got the ball back and kicked a field goal. With 2:12 left to play the game was tied.

But it took only one play for the Rams to erase our momentum. On first down after the kickoff, Warner launched a rainbow pass to Isaac Bruce, who cut back to catch the ball and eluded two of our defenders. He went all the way to the end zone, a seventy-three-yard touchdown. We were down again, 23–16.

After the kickoff and a penalty against us, we had the ball on our twelve-yard line. The clock showed 1:48. After the intensity of the playoffs, the week before the Super Bowl, and the game itself, I was exhausted—more tired than I'd ever been on a football field. Yet I could see and feel that the Rams defense was in even worse shape. We'd been hammering them with one rush after another. They were done.

We're going to find a way, I thought. *We're going to get this thing to overtime and we're going to win it.*

With the help of a couple of big scrambles by Steve and a face mask penalty, we marched into St. Louis territory. Rams players were so wiped out that they walked off the field. Dick Vermeil, the St. Louis coach, couldn't believe it, saying "You're taking yourself out of the game with twenty-six seconds to go?"

From the St. Louis twenty-six-yard line, Steve made an incredible play, escaping a near tackle by Kevin Carter and Jay Williams and passing to Kevin Dyson. We called a time-out. With six seconds left, we had the ball on the Rams' ten-yard line.

Time for one last play.

Yeah, I thought, *this is why we went through all those tough years.* It all pointed to and prepared us for this opportunity, this moment.

The play call was a pass. The man I needed to block, Jeff Zgonina, wasn't normally a pass rusher, but he was fresh off the bench. Usually, I would back up into pass protection, but knowing how dog-tired I was and that he would have more energy, I went after him from the snap of the ball, almost like it was a run block.

In the last game of the regular season, we'd scored a touchdown against Pittsburgh with the same play, a pass to Frank Wycheck in the end zone. This time Frank released from the line of scrimmage and Rams linebacker Mike Jones went with him. That left the middle of the field open for Kevin Dyson, who was running a slant from the right. Steve read it and made the pass to Kevin.

But Jones anticipated what was happening. As the pass was being thrown, he broke away from Frank toward Dyson. Kevin caught the ball inside the five-yard line and flashed toward the end zone, but Jones got his hands around Kevin's waist. As Kevin was going down, he stretched out his arm and the football toward the goal line. He was a few inches short.

It was right in front of me. I saw Dyson tackled, saw him stretch out his arm, saw that he didn't make it. One Yard Short, as the play is now known. I knew the game was over. I walked right past Kevin on the ground, through the end zone, and into the tunnel to the locker room. I didn't look back.

Man. What a letdown.

As disappointed as I was, though, I quickly realized that I wasn't as devastated as I expected to be. I had given everything I had, as had my teammates. I was proud of our effort and our team. I felt less like we'd lost and more like we'd just run out of time. What's more, it had been a fantastic season. We'd hung together through our wilderness years and forged a bond and a toughness because of them. We'd been behind in every single playoff game, as well as in the Super Bowl, and come back each time. This team did not quit.

I suddenly felt blessed to be part of it all. So often in sports and in life, the pursuit—the hunt—is actually more gratifying than the reward. Mike Jones later said as much: "The Super Bowl was the icing on the cake, but it's always the journey. Not necessarily when you get there, but the journey getting to the Super Bowl is the best part about it."

We might not have pulled off the miracle comeback this time, but I'd enjoyed every minute of the ride. I wouldn't trade those memories for anything.

16

GAME OVER

Of all the stratagems, to know when to quit is the best.
CHINESE PROVERB

I WAS FIRED UP ABOUT THE 2000 season. We had a great team and had just come as close as you can come without winning it all. I felt we were ready to close the deal.

Yes, I was thirty-nine years old. If I were a doctor or lawyer I'd be just entering my prime years, but when you're playing football at thirty-nine they start measuring you for a rocking chair. Yet I felt great. I'd thought about retirement but saw no reason to stop now. When I reported to training camp, I briefly wondered if I still had the skills and desire to get the job done. But once I got in the locker room and onto the practice field with the guys, I felt like I was twenty-one again, just like every season. I had a new crop of rookies to introduce to my dumb jokes and smack talk. I still felt I belonged.

Even though I was one of the old guys, I kept my youthful outlook by continuing to find ways to keep the game fun. In my early years with the Oilers, I enjoyed a touch football game I played with the offensive linemen on Mondays to work out the soreness from the game the day before. I also organized and sometimes invented games for my teammates: Helmet Master (borrowed from our quarterbacks), which involved setting down two helmets ten yards apart and tossing a football at them for points; Monkey in the Middle, essentially with a football; and the aforementioned Punt Master. In my quest to always triumph over my fellow Titans, I was sometimes accused of altering the rules to help my cause—don't ask me why.

My homemade competitions extended to the locker room (Ball Master) and weight room, though I'm not sure why I bothered on the weights. I wasn't strong enough to beat Munch and several of the others.

We started that season with a 16–13 loss to Buffalo—the Bills and their crowd were fired up for revenge after the Music City Miracle. The next game in Kansas City was miserable, eighty degrees, and incredibly humid. During warmups, center Kevin Long had to get a gash on his arm treated in the locker room, so I did all the pregame snaps. I was worn out before the game even started. Before every down I told myself, "All right, one more play, then you can take yourself out." I never did come out, but my body was definitely complaining.

We beat the Chiefs 17–14 and were 3–1 when we traveled to Cincinnati to play the Bengals. By this time I had a couple of streaks going—201 consecutive regular-season starts and seventeen-plus years, my entire career, without missing a game due to injury. Both of those achievements had been in jeopardy three years prior, however. Early in a game at Pittsburgh, a defensive end fell against my left knee.

I thought I was okay, but when I broke out of our next huddle, I realized something was wrong. I had to leave the game.

I had a second-degree strain of my medial collateral ligament (MCL). I took a lot of pride in those streaks, but it appeared they were over. Everyone assumed I would miss the next game at Seattle. Still, I hadn't quite given up hope. Maybe it'll get better. Maybe there's still a chance.

My knee was a little better on that Wednesday. By Friday, it actually felt pretty good. Since college I'd always worn knee braces, but the staff now provided me with a new one, which offered even more support. I was getting more optimistic. Jeff Fisher called me into his office and said, "Look, don't feel bad if your streak is over."

"Jeff, if I can't play up to my abilities, I won't play," I said. "But if it still feels the way it does now, I'd like to give it a try." I was a little apprehensive during Sunday warmups, but I did go the whole way against the Seahawks and played a decent game.

In the 2000 game in Cincinnati, it happened to me again, this time to the right knee. The diagnosis was the same, a second-degree MCL strain. But this time I knew I'd be able to play on it. In fact, the following week against Jacksonville was one of my better games. We beat the Jaguars, 27–13, to go 5–1.

Our winning streak stretched to eight, including a 14–6 triumph at Baltimore. The only score in the second half of that game was by our linebacker, Randall Godfrey, on an interception he returned for a touchdown. But when we hosted the Ravens in November they got us back, scoring on a touchdown pass with twenty-five seconds left to win 24–23. It was the first time we'd lost in Adelphia Coliseum.

The Jaguars also slipped by us in our second game with them,

16–13, but we finished the season strong, winning our last four. The final two games were shutouts, including a 31–0 thrashing of the Cowboys in the finale on Christmas night. Our defense was outstanding.

Jeff tried to give me a special moment in that Dallas game. In all the years I'd played football in high school, college, and the pros, I'd never scored a point. Jeff's plan if we got into the red zone (twenty yards from the Cowboys' goal line) was for me to line up at tight end and run a route into the back of the end zone.

He'd actually tried once before, in 1995 against Kansas City. The idea then was that after we scored a touchdown, I'd line up at center in a swinging-gate formation, where just the holder, kicker Rich Camarillo, and I were on the right side of the field. I'd snap the ball, take a couple steps into the end zone, turn around, and catch a two-point conversion pass from Rich. When Jeff told me about it, I thought, *Let's just kick the point after touchdown. Or let's run the ball. I don't need this stress in my life.* I appreciated what Jeff was doing, but my mentality—which is true of most offensive linemen—was that I didn't need to be the center of attention. I just wanted to quietly do my job well.

Back in 1995, the play nearly worked—Rich zinged the pass right at my chest—but at the last moment, a Chiefs player dove to knock the ball away.

But before the 2000 game against the Cowboys, I tried to talk Jeff out of his plan, without success. Sure enough, in the second quarter, we had a first-and-goal at the Dallas one-yard line—time for Jeff's trick play. I was nervous as I lined up at tight end. We probably would have fooled the Cowboys, but one of their linebackers, Barron Wortham, had been a Titan the season before. He pointed at me just before the snap and shouted, "Hey, Bruce is in at tight end—watch him! It's a trick play!"

I panicked. Instead of running all the way to the back of the end zone, I cut the route short, which allowed Wortham to cover me easily. I'm sure Steve McNair had been coached to throw the ball to me no matter what, but when he did, Wortham stepped in front of me and intercepted it. Apparently, it wasn't my destiny to appear in any NFL scoring logs.

But I was more upset by something that happened later in the game. I'd been performing well, throwing guys around. I thought, *Who needs to retire?* I could play two or three more years the way this game's going. Then on a play just before halftime, right guard Benji Olson and the man he was blocking fell on the back of my right heel. It felt as if my foot had broken in half. I had turf toe—I'd sprained the ligaments around the joint of my big toe. It was bad. This was one time when I wouldn't have been able to play the next week.

Once again, however, we'd finished the season with a stellar 13–3 record. It was the best in the NFL that year, so we had a first-round playoff bye, giving me some time to heal. That was a good thing, because our opponent would be the always dangerous Baltimore Ravens.

●　●　●

Since Carrie and the kids had missed part of our run to the Super Bowl the year before, I wanted to make sure that didn't happen this time. Thanks to the fact that we'd clinched home-field advantage throughout the playoffs, I told them we were all staying in Nashville until the end. I wanted them to enjoy the experience. That was especially true for Steven, now fifteen, and Kevin, thirteen. At this point, they were fully invested Titans fans. This was going to be fun.

My teammates and I knew the Ravens were a tough opponent with a great defense. I was also still dealing with my turf toe, which required an injection before the game. But I'm sure that we were confident that we were the better team and that we'd find a way to beat them. This was just the first step toward our destiny.

The game was of course a sellout, played under cloudy skies. We got the ball first and did exactly what we set out to do. Eddie George rushed six times for thirty-two yards on an eleven-play drive that ended with Eddie's two-yard touchdown. It wasn't easy, but I felt we were executing well and moving their line. I never would have guessed that that would be our only touchdown of the day.

The Ravens answered in the second quarter when quarterback Trent Dilfer hit a wide-open Shannon Sharpe on a fifty-six-yard pass, which led to a one-yard touchdown run. It would be the last offensive touchdown by either team. I didn't know it then, but this game would be decided by the special teams.

We should have had the lead at halftime. Our field goal attempt with 2:27 to play in the second quarter was blocked by the Ravens' Keith Washington. Then Chris Coleman made a block of his own of a Baltimore punt, giving us the ball on the Ravens' twenty-five-yard line with 1:44 to go. But we stalled on the thirteen-yard line. This time, Al Del Greco's kick hit the left upright and bounced away. We'd missed on two huge opportunities.

The start of the third quarter felt like some weird déjà vu. Coleman again blocked a Ravens punt and we again stalled just short of the Baltimore goal line. Al connected on this kick, however, giving us a

10–7 lead. But the Ravens came back with their own field goal to tie the game with three minutes left in the period.

Going into the fourth quarter, I knew we'd outgained Baltimore and had great field position most of the game. We'd had opportunities. We just needed to stop making mistakes, keep pounding the ball, and play like the great team I knew we were.

Yet somehow, thanks to two plays, it all unraveled.

The first came after Steve tried to run for a first down and was a yard short at the Baltimore twenty-five-yard line. On our field goal attempt, Washington got his hand on a kick for the second time that day. The ball was deflected to Baltimore's Anthony Mitchell, who caught it on the ten-yard line, ran down the right sideline, cut back to the middle, and scored—a ninety-yard return for a touchdown.

I still expected us to come back. With just under seven minutes left to play, we had the ball near midfield. But when Steve threw a pass to Eddie, the ball arrived just slightly behind him. It bounced off his right shoulder. With the ball still in the air, both Eddie and Ray Lewis fought for it. Lewis came away with it, eluded tacklers, and ran fifty yards for another defensive touchdown. Eddie just lay there, facedown. I don't think he could stand to watch it. Frankly, neither could I.

Despite outgaining the Ravens, 317 yards to 134, we lost the game, 24–10. Our ride to the Super Bowl had ended almost before it started. Baltimore would go on to become world champions, defeating the New York Giants in the Super Bowl, 34–7.

It was the most painful loss of my career. I had fully expected us to win. What made it even tougher was how hard it was on the kids. It felt like a loss for the whole family. Instead of enjoying a special time together we were suddenly packing to go back to Houston. I had to give the Ravens credit, though. Their defense was the best I ever played against.

●   ●   ●

I had a much more pleasant duty to perform that summer. Munch had just been elected to the NFL Hall of Fame. He asked me to introduce him before his induction speech, which I still consider one of the great honors of my career. I told the crowd in Canton, Ohio, "He set a standard of excellence that myself and every offensive lineman who played with him has tried to emulate. The hits that he put on linebackers were legendary. Words like integrity, excellence, and honor come to mind. Mike Munchak epitomizes that to me both on the field and off, and I don't think that there could be a better person to represent these values than him. Not only as a player but as a husband, a father, and especially as a friend."

Jackie Slater was inducted that year too. It was a special weekend, one I appreciated even more because it allowed me to miss the first few days of training camp.

I hadn't made any decision about my future going into the 2001 season. I still enjoyed playing and still believed we had a good team. But more and more, thoughts about retirement crept into my mind. The loss to the Ravens had certainly left a bad taste in my mouth, but I was bothered more by the impact of our two-city life on my family. I knew it wasn't easy for the kids, especially Steven since he was now a junior in high school, to go to school a half year in Nashville and the other half in Houston. Then there was my turf toe. It was better but it hadn't gone away. It felt like someone had stuck an ice pick in there.

I was also bothered by hearing young players grumble about this or that. I'd think, *Most guys would kill to be in our shoes. We get paid well to play this game we love. Why are you complaining?*

On September 9 we opened the season with a loss to the Miami Dolphins. Two days later, terrorists launched the 9/11 attacks on America. I remember praying with my kids and reminding them that God was in control. Besides being a terrible tragedy, it was a big-time perspective check. I thought, *The NFL has been such a huge part of your life. You've treated it like it's life and death.* But life is so much bigger than football. It made me wonder if I needed to shift my priorities.

We lost two more games to drop to 0–3, already as many defeats as we'd recorded over the entire season the year before. We hosted Tampa Bay next. You never expect to hear something nice from your opponents, especially at the start of a game. But when I went onto the field for our first possession, the Bucs' All-Pro defensive tackle, Warren Sapp, startled me by saying, "Man, I got a lot of respect for what you've done all these years."

I didn't want to hear those words at that moment. Before every NFL game, you build up a level of antagonism toward your opponent that gets you ready to play. Now Warren Sapp was complimenting me? Oh man, I do not want to like this guy. After the game, fine. But not now.

We beat Tampa Bay, 31–28, but it was a rough game for me. The heat sapped my energy and my ankle got rolled up. I wasn't happy with my performance. Nagging injuries, lousy play, and tributes from opposing players? I suddenly felt old.

The feeling intensified three weeks later in a Monday night game against the Steelers in their new stadium, Heinz Field. When we broke the huddle for our first play, I looked across the line at their heralded rookie, nose tackle Casey Hampton. I did the math—he was five years old when I reported to my first NFL training camp.

Man, I'm old.

Our team must have been feeling old too. Our pass defense wasn't nearly as strong and the offense wasn't quite as efficient. Our record was only 5–7 when we hosted Green Bay in December. I'd begun the season at left guard and later moved to center, but by the Packers game I was back to starting at left guard. In both positions I'd struggled, at least by my standards. But in the cooler weather I finally put together a strong performance. We beat Green Bay and Brett Favre, 26–20.

Our next game was in Oakland. In the second quarter I tweaked my groin, something I'd never done before. Neither team could get going on offense. It was still a scoreless tie when I put my helmet on and got ready to walk onto the field for our first possession of the second half.

Suddenly a feeling of panic set in. *I can't move!* The tightness in my groin had gotten worse.

I turned to Munch. "Hey," I said. "You better put (Zach) Piller in for me."

Under a light rain, I stood on the sidelines with the defense and reserves and watched my team drive down the field without me. The Raiders fans, especially those wearing wild costumes colored silver and black in the notorious section known as the Black Hole, yelled for their defense to stop us.

Suddenly it hit me. You know what? Your body's breaking down. This is it. This is your last year.

During a lull in the action, I again approached Munch. "Hey," I said. "I'm done. I'm through." He knew what I was saying. I think it surprised us both. It was strange to say it and strange to mean it.

On January 6, 2002, we hosted the Cincinnati Bengals in my final game. I hadn't announced anything officially but the team knew what was happening. Earlier that week, Jeff asked me for a list of songs so his daughter could create a playlist for our pregame warmup. On game day, the scoreboard read, "Music provided by Bruce Matthews." I'd picked songs like "He Ain't Heavy, He's My Brother" by the Hollies, which were completely out of character for what we usually did. It was pretty funny.

Going into the game, I wasn't sure exactly how I wanted to end my playing career. Then, on our first drive, Steve McNair threw a forty-one-yard bomb down the left sideline to Derrick Mason for a touchdown. "Hey Munch," I said as we celebrated on the sideline, "to have that as my last play, it can't get any better than that." It was my final down on offense. I still snapped for point-after-touchdowns, so my last official play in the NFL was a successful extra point at the end of the third quarter. That score gave us a 21–20 lead. Unfortunately, as had happened too often in my career, the Bengals came back with a field goal in the final seconds. They beat us, 23–21.

As I ran off the field, I thought about how I'd been playing football since I was a little boy. It was weird to think it was over. But I had no regrets about how my career had turned out. Very few guys have the opportunity to make a career in the NFL, let alone avoid serious injury, play for great teams with great teammates, and stay in the game for nineteen years.

I'd said it before and I'd keep on saying it, because there was no other way to describe it. I'd been blessed.

17

THE BIGGER PICTURE

For I know the plans I have for you . . .
plans to give you hope and a future.

JEREMIAH 29:11

IF I NEEDED ANY MORE REMINDERS that some things in life are more important than football, I got one just three weeks after playing my last game. I was at home after spending the day with the family celebrating Mikey's eighth birthday. The phone rang. Dad had remarried after Mom passed away, and it was Carolyn who was calling.

My brother Brad had just passed away.

It was hard to believe. I knew Brad had been dealing with health issues recently—he'd had health struggles for years—but I thought he'd pull through, like he always had in the past. His body had finally worn out.

Back in the eighties, both Brad and Ray had been doing great. They lived in adjoining apartments in Arcadia near my sister, Kristy. Ray worked in maintenance at the data-tape division of Kodak, and

Brad was an assembler for an electrical company. They could read and write, shop for groceries, cook, handle their checking accounts, and get around on the city bus system.

After work on Friday, September 30, 1988, Brad was walking to the Arcadia High School track to do his usual three-mile run. He stepped into a crosswalk and a guy driving a pickup ran a red light. The collision sent Brad flying forty feet.

Doctors said he might not survive. They gave him twenty-six pints of blood but he never lost consciousness. I didn't find out about the accident until after my game that Sunday—Dad didn't want to distract me. Following our Monday practice, Carrie came to pick me up and deliver the news in person. I was driving when she told me. I had to pull off the road to compose myself.

On my off day that week, I flew out to visit Brad. It was a tough sight. He had a halo brace around his head and a tube down his throat, so he couldn't talk. He'd undergone a tracheotomy, a colostomy, and a gastrostomy. He was stabilized, but the accident had left Brad a quadriplegic—he was paralyzed from the neck down.

It was such a terrible blow to a guy who already faced so many challenges. "Why, God?" I later prayed. "You've blessed me and my family so much. Why are Brad and Ray the way they are? What did Brad do to deserve this?"

Our family supported Brad, as well as Ray, the best we could. Kristy visited Brad in the hospital every day for nearly a year. Carrie and I and the rest of the family came to see Brad when possible as well. Bruz and Leslie often invited Ray over for dinner and to spend the night.

I'd be apprehensive before my visits with Brad, thinking, *How is this thing going to go?* I was afraid I'd see him in a bad state and not be able to encourage him. Yet by the time I had to leave, I was the one who felt encouraged. Brad always said, "I'm doing all right." I was amazed that he wasn't bitter, that he never gave into the temptation to complain.

When Carrie and I talked to Brad about God, I began to understand where that positive attitude came from. In the Bible, Jesus said, "I tell you the truth, anyone who will not receive the kingdom of God like a little child will never enter it" (Luke 18:17). Brad already had that childlike faith in the Lord. After the accident, it grew stronger. It seemed to me that whatever Brad lost physically, he gained in awareness of the bigger picture. He might not have been able to articulate it, but it was as if he understood that life was temporary and that, even with his difficulties, he had much to be grateful for.

Even after doctors had to amputate his leg, Brad continued to encourage and inspire not just me but so many people he came in contact with. Once he said, "It was God's plan for me to get injured this way." That blew me away. I don't know that I could have responded to so many challenges with the same level of faith and trust. But that was Brad.

I still miss my brother today. I'm fortunate, though, that Ray lives in a group home near us in Texas. He visits us on holidays and, every couple of weeks, we'll go to a movie or have a burger together. Whenever we see him, he's got lots of stories for us. It doesn't matter if we've heard them before—he's going to tell them again. Brad was probably more in touch with his spiritual side, but Ray also has a belief and trust in God. I'm so grateful for both those guys, and can't imagine what my life would have been without them.

● ● ●

I also couldn't have imagined what was in store for our family in 2003. Carrie and I had planned on having only six kids, but we discovered that God had a different agenda. Carrie was pregnant again.

We were both in our forties and knew there was some risk of complications. Carrie's bloodwork showed there was an increased chance that our baby would have Down syndrome. A doctor wanted to perform amniocentesis so we'd know for sure, but since an ultrasound hadn't picked up any health issues, we decided against it. Even though any danger from the amnio was small, we figured the procedure just wasn't necessary. We were having this baby and would take whatever we got.

Not that we were seeking a special-needs child. We both prayed that our baby would be healthy, with no complications. Carrie had such peace throughout her pregnancy that we figured God had answered our prayers.

Our seventh child—and second daughter—was born by Cesarean section on November 18: Gwendolyn Gracie Rose Matthews. It was a relief when the doctor announced that our baby didn't have Down syndrome.

Our relief was short-lived. Carrie asked, "Are you sure she doesn't have Down syndrome?"

"I'm sure," the doctor said. "I checked the palms of her hands" (a single, deep crease in the palm can be a sign of Down syndrome).

A moment later, a nurse showed Gwenie to Carrie for the first time. Sometimes a mother's intuition—maybe most of the time—supersedes a doctor's training. "Yes," Carrie said immediately, "she does have Down syndrome."

Another doctor soon confirmed Carrie's statement.

I'd known it was a possibility. Even so, the reality of her condition stunned me. My mind flashed to all the special moments I thought my new daughter would miss out on: going to the prom, getting married, having a family. Her life had just begun and I was already mourning her future. Down syndrome? It just didn't seem right.

Before I could think more about the future, though, we had to get through the first day. The hospital staff took Gwenie to the Neonatal Intensive Care Unit because so many Down syndrome babies have serious health issues, including heart or intestinal problems requiring surgery. I hoped and prayed she'd be all right.

The next day brought good news: Gwenie was healthy as a horse. She was doing great, but her parents were still reeling.

Carrie had always turned the birth of each of our children into a celebration. She would decorate her hospital room with banners and garlands, put on a fancy robe, and get out a picnic basket that she'd packed ahead of time. I'd come in with the kids and we'd have a little party. As she lay in bed on the morning after Gwenie's birth, however, partying wasn't on her mind.

"What am I going to do with a special-needs child?" she worried. "How am I going to care for her when I have six other kids?"

In the next instant, though, Carrie made an important decision— she would celebrate Gwenie just as much as she'd celebrated the rest of her children. Gwenie wouldn't be shortchanged just because she had Down syndrome. In a way, it was like the decision my mom and dad made so many years before about Brad and Ray—they would be treated exactly the same as their siblings.

You better get up and do what you do, Carrie thought. *One day, you'll look back on this moment, look at the pictures, and be so glad that you celebrated her.*

Later that morning, when I showed up at the hospital with the kids, Carrie was in her party robe and the room was decorated just like always. We have pictures from that day of everyone in the family holding Gwenie. In each one, our smiles stretch from ear to ear.

We may have given Gwenie a proper welcome into the family, but I still struggled with adjusting to our new reality. I went through a month of feeling depressed for her and us before I began to remember that God had a plan for Gwenie, just as He did for the rest of my family.

It wasn't easy for Carrie either, especially since she took on most of the responsibility of caring for our new addition. As Gwenie got older, we realized how much we took for granted with our other kids. Gwenie is mostly nonverbal. She speaks only a few words, so communication can be a challenge. She needs help with bathing, and someone always has to be with her. Carrie invests an enormous amount of time in caring for Gwenie. I appreciate my wife so much for that.

Yet I know we both feel that the joys Gwenie brings us far outweigh the hard work. For instance, in many ways she's an easy child—she doesn't complain and is nearly always content. She gives me something to look forward to every school-day morning. When I'm reading in my recliner, Gwenie will come downstairs, grab a box of each of her two favorite cereals—Cocoa Puffs and Cinnamon Toast Crunch—and give me a hug, crushing the boxes between us. She has her priorities—a girl needs to eat breakfast, after all—yet she makes sure to fit Dad in too.

Hugs are one of Gwenie's special talents. I remember walking into

Houston's NRG Stadium with some of the family to see one of the boys' football games. All of a sudden, Gwenie broke away from us and ran up to a security guard who wasn't much taller than Gwenie. The security guard, startled, put her hands up and said, "Whoa, easy." But once she looked at Gwenie, her hands dropped. Gwenie gave the woman a big hug.

"Thank you so much," the woman said to Gwenie, smiling. "I really needed that today."

That happens all the time. Gwenie may be lacking in some areas, but it's almost as if she has a sixth sense for people who are hurting and need encouragement. Though a few are surprised at first, hardly anyone turns down a hug when Gwenie approaches them. It's amazing how often she picks someone out who responds just like that security guard.

In some ways, I'm envious of my daughter. She makes no pretense and has no worries. She doesn't care if her shirt doesn't match her shorts, if her hair's out of place, or if she has a chocolate milk goatee after eating her Cocoa Puffs. For her, life is all about loving and being loved. Nothing else matters.

I often take Gwenie swimming, which used to be her favorite thing to do. But her new favorite thing is going to dance class. When Carrie asks if she wants to dance, she races upstairs with Carrie to get dressed, runs back down, grabs her dance bag, and is raring to go. When she performs in a recital, you can tell she has no butterflies or cares—she frolics and leaps with unmistakable joy. If she makes a mistake, she just laughs. If she breaks out of the line to do something original, who cares?

I wish I lived with that sense of abandon and freedom.

When our family goes out in public, Gwenie is more comfortable than I am. I'm usually the one that reaches for her hand, not the other way around. She's my security blanket.

Maybe what I'm most thankful for is the impact Gwenie's had on our family and even extended family. Simply put, Gwenie offers unconditional love. She's showed us how to love and appreciate each other more. She's also taught us to have even greater compassion for people who aren't like us.

> *My dad told me when Gwenie was born that all she wants to do is love and be loved. She's so innocent. When you're in a room with her, she smiles and you smile too. She's been so good for our family.*
>
> JAKE MATTHEWS

Apparently Gwenie's impact extends even beyond our family. Once, a bunch of people were standing in a line at a Houston-area mall. One of the little boys in line was a special-needs kid and some of his older siblings were treating him badly.

Another boy there happened to be Max Queen, son of my old friend from California, Bob Queen. The Queens had moved to Houston years ago. When Max saw what was going on, he spoke up. "My friends have a daughter with Down syndrome," he said, "and they don't treat her like that."

It's amazing, sometimes, what our kids can teach us.

I know that many parents do not choose to keep their babies if they discover during pregnancy that they have Down syndrome. As the technology for detection has advanced over the years, abortion rates for Down syndrome babies have increased. I can't help wondering if those moms and dads see our family when we're out in public and notice this beautiful little girl and how loving we all are with each other. What do they think? Is it painful? Do they have regrets?

I never would have asked for a Down syndrome child, but now I can't imagine not having Gwenie or her being anyone other than who she is. Carrie feels the same way. Once when Gwenie was nearly eighteen months old, she and Carrie were lying on our family-room floor, just enjoying some time together. It was April 5, 2005. Carrie thought, *I have so much to do. I need to get up and get to work.* In the next instant, however, her attitude changed. *But I just don't care. I don't want to get up. I just want to lie here and play with this little baby.*

That's when she had an epiphany: *Gwenie did not come to be a burden. Gwenie came to free me from my burdens.*

> *Most people don't understand what a blessing it is to have someone in your life with special needs. From afar, it can seem like a burden. But you wouldn't believe the amount of unconditional love Gwenie gives. She's not influenced by the outside world; everything she does is based from good. She's the most liked of all the Matthews, because she's so pure. It's humbling to be around her.*
>
> CLAY MATTHEWS III (GWENIE'S COUSIN)

The more I'm around Gwenie, the easier it is for me to see God's hand in all of this. It's as if He's saying, "Look, you leave all the heavy lifting to Me. You quit trying to figure it out. Just trust Me." She has helped me come to terms with my questions about Brad's hard life and, like

Brad, see the bigger picture. The Lord had a purpose for Brad that included encouraging me and others. God took care of him in this life, and He's still taking care of him, just as He's taking care of me and Gwenie and my family.

When I first learned that Gwenie had Down syndrome, I definitely did not think of it as a blessing. I could not have been more wrong. She brings me love and joy every day. Without doubt, she is one of the greatest blessings of my life.

18

CALL ME COACH

Team spirit means you are willing to sacrifice personal considerations for the welfare of all. That defines a team player.

JOHN WOODEN

FOOTBALL IS A TEAM GAME. THAT may be an obvious statement that applies to many sports, but it's most true of football. No other major sports carry more players on their team rosters. An NFL squad is made up of fifty-three active players and maybe twenty coaches, and each one has a role. The quarterback and head coach may get a disproportionate amount of the glory for the team's victories, but the truth is that neither succeeds unless everyone else does his job. When any one of those players or coaches starts to put his own needs ahead of the team's, everything starts to unravel.

That was one of the lessons I learned from my dad when I was a kid, and saw played out in high school, college, and the pros. It was something I tried to pass on to my kids. But I never expected to do it in an official role after I retired as a player. Unlike many of my peers, I planned to stay far away from coaching.

My resolve came from that year living alone in Tennessee in 1997, when I got my first close-up view of the NFL coaching life. I watched Munch put in long hours week after week as the Titans' offensive line coach. Since my apartment was closer to our practice facility than his house, he'd show up on Tuesday night—or sometimes, at two or three on Wednesday morning—to crash with me, then get up at six the next morning to go back. After seeing that all season, I said, "Heck, no, I ain't doing that."

I still felt that way in fall 2002, the beginning of my first season as a football spectator. That's when my old friend Bob Queen approached me. Bob's son and Mikey, who was eight, were going to be on the same youth football team, the First Colony Broncos. Bob and two other dads I knew from Little League, Jeff Ebarb and Barin Wise, were the coaches. "Hey," Bob said, "the guys would love to have you involved. What do you think?"

"Nah," I said. "I don't want to do the coaching thing. I'm just going to watch." Then, I thought about it for a minute. "Maybe I could sit in on your first meeting. Just to see what's going on."

At the meeting, somebody mentioned using the wishbone, an offense that had been out-of-date for decades. *Oh, my gosh*, I thought. *I can't sit by and have my boy run the wishbone.*

"All right," I said, "I'll coach the offensive line. But we'll run my offense."

Coaching eight- and nine-year-olds was like herding cats, but I thoroughly enjoyed it. It's rewarding to watch a kid try to do what you tell him and have success, to see that switch flip on in his mind when he believes in what you're teaching him. It was also great developing friendships with the other dads. I ended up coaching that team with those guys for the next four years. To my surprise, I was hooked.

I did suffer one letdown during my second year with that team. I was throwing passes to the kids before a practice. It had rained recently and the ground was muddy and slick. I slipped, felt my knee pop, and went down. For nineteen years in the NFL, my knees had held up beautifully. Apparently coaching was more hazardous to my health—I'd torn a quad tendon and needed knee surgery.

After Mikey moved on to a junior high–level team, I agreed to coach Luke's grade school–age team. Then Sid Smith, a former USC offensive lineman and first-round NFL draft pick, asked me to be the offensive coordinator at a local Christian high school. I said yes. Between the two teams, I was suddenly coaching five hours a day. Jake was going to be a high school freshman the next season. *If I'm going to work this hard at coaching,* I thought, *I might as well coach my own kids.*

According to district policy at Elkins High, where Jake was headed, you couldn't coach as a volunteer. You had to be a full-time member of the staff. Since there was an opening, I applied for and was hired as a full-time substitute teacher at the high school. I went into that experience with a zero-tolerance policy. I figured if kids didn't want to learn, then I didn't need them in the classroom. My thinking soon changed. I found out that some of the kids came from homes with distant and verbally abusive parents. It was no wonder they acted out at school. They just wanted attention and to know that someone cared. My heart softened toward them. When possible, I sat down with them, listened, and tried to give them advice. It reinforced what

I already believed as a coach, that most players and people don't need to be yelled at for motivation. They just want to be around someone who cares about them and wants to help them get better.

At Elkins, I was head coach of the freshman team. Jake was our quarterback. I also helped with the varsity offensive line and ran the end-zone camera. I coached there for three seasons, which included Jake's junior year and Mikey's freshman year. Once again, even though I put in a lot of hours, I enjoyed it tremendously. I decided I wanted to try my hand at the highest level.

By this time the NFL had put a new franchise in Houston, the Texans. Their coach was Gary Kubiak. I had played with Gary back in the 1983 Hula Bowl, a college all-star game held in Hawaii, and gotten to know him then. I asked if I could join the staff, so that I could learn the ropes. I told Gary I'd do the grunt work, whatever they needed. That's just what happened. For the 2009 and 2010 seasons, I was the Texans' offensive quality-control coach. I wrote up and stuffed playbooks, coached the show team, and helped with the offensive line. I learned a ton.

Being part of Gary's staff was a great situation for me, since I was able to coach in the NFL and still live at my home in Houston. I had no desire to chase higher-responsibility jobs around the league and uproot my family. I anticipated staying with the Texans for the foreseeable future.

Right after the 2010 season, Bruz flew to Houston and the two of us drove to Mobile, Alabama, to watch his son Casey practice for the Senior Bowl, another college all-star contest. Casey had just finished an outstanding career as a linebacker at the University of Oregon and had played in the national championship game earlier in January.

Munch, who still coached for the Titans, was also in Mobile to evaluate talent for the upcoming draft. We started talking. "Hey," he said to me, "if I ever get a head-coaching job, I want you to be my offensive-line coach."

"Yeah, sure," I said. I treated it more as a joke than a serious possibility. NFL head-coaching offers don't exactly pop up every day, even for someone as qualified as Munch. I didn't give it another thought.

After a couple days in Mobile, Bruz and I got in my car to drive back to Houston. We had just gotten underway on I-10 and were relaxing and observing all the casino billboards when a radio broadcaster announced breaking news: the Titans had just fired Jeff Fisher.

It was one of those moments where time seemed to stop. Never in a million years did I think Jeff would be let go. I felt bad for him. I also had the sudden feeling that Munch's invitation had just taken on new significance.

Sure enough, within ten days Munch interviewed for, was offered, and accepted the job as head coach of the Titans. He repeated his offer to me, and this time it was no joke.

Mikey was in his junior year of high school at the time. We wouldn't move him with only one year of school left, which meant Carrie and rest of the family wouldn't move either. As attractive as the opportunity was for me to coach for Munch, I did not want to leave my family and Houston. I'd done that once already and knew how tough it would be.

"Carrie," I said, "give me a reason not to do this."

"You've got to do this," she said. "You'll regret it for the rest of your life if you don't go up there and coach with Mike."

I realized she was right. Though a month earlier I couldn't have imagined it, I was once again going to be a Titan.

● ● ●

Coaching is all about helping players get better. I told the Titans offensive linemen, "I've had the benefit of playing with some great players and being coached by some great coaches. I'm confident that what I'm teaching you here will help you. But if you have a suggestion or know a better way to do it, I'm all ears."

Most of the guys were receptive to that approach. Once they realize you have their best interests at heart, most players are more than willing to let you help them along the journey. That relationship with the players and the opportunity to see them get the most out of their talent is what makes coaching so rewarding.

One of my goals going into coaching in the NFL was to speak to players as a mentor, not only to help them improve their performance on the field but also to offer some guidance for life off the field. For the most part, that turned out to be unrealistic. The hours for an NFL coach are crazy. A typical schedule during the season might be Monday, seven in the morning to ten at night; Tuesday, seven in the morning until midnight; Wednesday, seven in the morning to ten at night; Thursday, seven in the morning to eight in the evening; Friday, seven in the morning to two in the afternoon; and Saturday, seven in the morning until eleven at night. Sunday was game day. There just wasn't time for one-on-one interaction with the players that went beyond football.

But one-on-one time was a different situation with the coaches.

We spent so many hours together that you couldn't help developing close relationships. I especially enjoyed getting to know an old nemesis from the Fiesta Bowl, Chet Parlavecchio, the former Penn State and NFL linebacker. The Titans coaches also held regular Bible studies that strengthened the bonds between us, and between us and the Lord. It was a great way to counteract the tremendous pressure that comes with coaching in the NFL.

Though I didn't get to know the players as well as I would have liked, I did already have a relationship with one player who was part of the organization for all three years I was with the Titans—my son Kevin.

When Kevin graduated from high school, he had a few scholarship offers to play center in college. Texas A&M didn't offer a scholarship, but he had a good feeling about the program from his visits there and decided to walk on. It's extremely rare for a walk-on to earn a college football scholarship, so I was pretty excited when he called me after a spring practice his freshman year to say the coaches were talking about it. Kevin did beat the odds, earning that scholarship his first year and starting at center his last two years. Though he went undrafted after graduating, that Matthews stubbornness kicked in again. He made the Titans practice squad and was added to the active roster late in the season. He played three games, starting the last one against the Colts.

We signed Kevin for the 2011 and 2012 seasons as well. During training camp in 2012, he was competing for a starting job when he suffered a concussion, missed practice time, and lost his opportunity. Kevin still played in every game and did earn that starting position for two games late in the season. Then he injured his ankle, ending his season.

I loved having Kevin on the team, but told him he wouldn't get any special treatment. "If you get to play, it won't be because I'm leading the charge," I said. "I'll put the interests of the team first." I know he expected nothing less. The players gave him a bad time after he called me Dad during one of our first meetings, but he handled the situation well. It might have been harder on me—it was nerve-racking for me when he played, as it always is when I'm watching one of my kids perform. I remember one game where J. J. Watt, the Texans' three-time NFL Defensive Player of the Year, drew two holding penalties on Kevin. As a dad it was stressful to watch, but as a coach I needed to put that aside and focus on how to prevent it from happening again. All in all, I was proud of the way Kevin battled that day.

In 2013, after the team had some injuries, we signed him again in November. He was released and re-signed several times that year, which is part of regular business for a team but always hard on the player. I respect the way Kevin handled all those ups and downs. To his credit, he was a professional throughout. He made me proud as a dad and a coach.

The Titans went 9–7 in my first year coaching them. We missed out on the playoffs, but were in the hunt until the final week. I enjoyed the experience, but living without my family was a grind. Once again, their absence reminded me how much they meant to me and how blessed I was to have them in my life. The next year, Mikey joined his brother Jake at Texas A&M (Kevin had paved the way, so they offered football scholarships to both from the start). With Mikey off to college, it allowed Carrie, Luke, and Gwenie to join me in Nashville. Even Marilyn moved up, landing a job at Vanderbilt and leasing an apartment. I was definitely happy to be back among the people I loved.

•   •   •

As a coach, I recognized more than ever that for both individual players and the organization to achieve their goals and win, everyone had to have a team-first attitude. There's a fine line between being selfish and being a team player. During contract negotiations, there's nothing wrong with touting your skills and accomplishments. At those moments, you need to prove your value to the team.

When you're talking about your coaches and teammates during the season, however, that's another matter. While addressing the media, some guys will rip their teammates for a poor performance or talk about how they need the ball more. That's a proven method for destroying team chemistry. Once you believe the guy next to you is interested only in himself, it becomes more tempting to adopt the same approach.

Eddie George was a guy who understood this and handled it flawlessly. Everything that came out of his mouth was "we," not "I." It may not have made great copy for the media, but it was important for promoting what we wanted to accomplish as a team. Steve McNair was the same way. There were plenty of times when he could have criticized those of us on the offensive line for allowing the defense to pressure him. It didn't happen. He just wanted to win and understood how to go about it.

These guys had what Bill Russell, the former Boston Celtics great and eleven-time National Basketball Association champion, calls "team ego." After he retired, Russell talked about it with a group of current NBA players: "Do you know the difference between your ego and mine?" he said. "My ego is not a personal ego, it's a team ego. My ego demands—for myself—the success of the team. My personal achievement became my team achievement."

I get what Russell means. During my career, individual awards were always nice, but nothing was more fulfilling than our run to the Super Bowl in 1999. The accomplishments of the team that season were what satisfied me most.

What goes for the players applies just as much to coaches. I've already talked about Buddy Ryan and the problems we had on the 1993 Oilers. That atmosphere was such a contrast with what I experienced while on the coaching staffs with the Texans and Titans. When individual ego rises above team goals, failure will soon follow. It was refreshing—but not surprising—to hear Gary Kubiak speak about his team after the Denver Broncos defeated Carolina in the fiftieth Super Bowl. He consistently deflected any praise for himself and commended his players and fellow coaches instead. When I heard that, I thought, *Yeah, that's the guy I was blessed to work with for two years.*

It was the same working with Munch. He had a no-nonsense approach. You weren't going to get a lot of fluff or funny one-liners out of him. He wasn't interested in trying to look good for the media. He was all about doing what was necessary to build up the team.

That first spring after I joined the Titans coaching staff, we drafted quarterback Jake Locker from the University of Washington with the eighth overall pick. He was a talented kid who fit the mold I'm talking about—team first. We believed he could be a leader for the franchise for years to come, and he won the starting job at the beginning of the

2012 season, but a series of injuries prevented him from reaching his potential. Thanks in part to the changes in personnel at quarterback, the team dropped to 6–10 in 2012 before going 7–9 in 2013.

Our owner, Bud Adams, died during that 2013 season. Although I believed in Munch's long-term plan and that the Titans were moving in the right direction, the new group calling the organization's shots felt otherwise. They wanted him to make changes to his program that he didn't agree with. Not surprisingly, Munch refused, saying he would only make changes that he thought were in the best interest of the team. It was another example of his integrity and the kind of person he is. Because he and the new leadership didn't have the same vision, they parted ways. Most of the assistant coaches were dismissed as well.

As far as I was concerned, letting Munch go was a big mistake by the Titans. Over the next two years, the team's record dropped to 2–14 in 2014 and 3–13 in 2015.

As Bum Phillips used to say, "There's two kinds of coaches, them that's fired and them that's gonna be fired." I was disappointed for Munch, the other coaches, and myself. But it didn't take me long to see the silver lining for me. I had more time for my family and to see my kids play. If this was God's plan for this season of my life, I needed to accept it.

I'd like to coach in the NFL again. I miss the competition, the relationships, and the opportunity to share from my experience. Maybe that will happen down the line and maybe it won't. I know that I gave it my best when I was doing it and I'm learning to be content with that.

19

LEGACY

---

*The reason I'm on this earth is to serve God; to be the best
husband, father, son, brother, and friend I can be; and to lead
people to Christ. These are the things that matter.*

TIM BROWN

ONE OF MY ALL-TIME FAVORITE MEMORIES is from a Saturday
in February 2007. I was driving home from a church men's retreat
when my phone rang. It was Carrie. I was in my first year of eligibility
for the NFL Hall of Fame and knew that the inductees would be announced that day. "Did I get in?" I asked.

"Yes!"

Hearing that report was great, but what I especially enjoyed was
how excited my family was. After I did a couple hours of media interviews, the phone lines cleared and I was able to call my dad.

"Dad," I said, "did you hear the news about the Hall of Fame?"

"No," he said, "did I make it in?"

I laughed. "No, you didn't."

"Yeah," he said, "I guess I'm no longer eligible." It was a typical

Dad joke, but I knew that underneath the humor he was proud of me.

I actually endured quite a bit of anxiety between the announcement and the induction ceremonies in August. I did not look forward to being in the spotlight for those three days in Canton, Ohio. Once I got there and stopped thinking about my reaction to everything, however, I saw how much my family, friends, and other football fans were enjoying the chance to celebrate the occasion with me. My anxiety disappeared.

It was a thrill to sit onstage before my induction speech and listen to Munch introduce me, just as I'd done for him six years before. "Competitive," Munch said, "is the word that best describes Bruce. His desire to be the best is unmatched. He wants to win at everything he does: a sport, a video game, even an argument. He can claim an opinion he doesn't even believe in just to see if he can still win the argument.

"Classic Bruce, though, is when you're in a car with him and a song comes on the radio. He immediately yells out the name of the song and the artist. He would say, 'Springsteen, "Glory Days," bam.' Even though no one else is playing this game, he's still competing. I think that Bruce's competitive spirit was his secret weapon and a reason why he played nineteen seasons. It kept him young at heart. He always found a way to make it fun, and it showed on the field every Sunday."

Munch was probably right. That combination of competitive spirit and pure enjoyment of the game kept me going. Who would have guessed where it would lead? As I said when I got up to the podium, "If someone had told me when I was a kid that one day I would play in the NFL, let alone be inducted in the Pro Football Hall of Fame, I wouldn't have believed them." To be part of a club that included Bart Starr, Gale Sayers, Deacon Jones, and other NFL greats I'd admired while growing up was an honor I never imagined.

Obviously, I'm proud of my football legacy. It's satisfying to realize that my fourteen consecutive Pro Bowls are tied for the most ever, to hold the record for games played by an offensive lineman (296), and to be a member of the NFL's 1990s All-Decade Team. More rewarding to me is that I never missed a game in my career due to injury.

What I value just as much are the memories of competing against the best. I had so much respect for All-Pro defensive linemen such as Bruce Smith, Too Tall Jones, Randy White, Howie Long, Reggie White, and John Randall. Those guys, as well as great team defenses like the Ravens, added a lot of stress to my life.

I remember one spring when the upcoming season schedule came out and I saw we would play the Raiders. Though the game was months away, I lay in bed that night until one or two in the morning, thinking, *Man, I know Howie Long's going to jump the snap count* (Howie was so good at timing the quarterback's signals and getting into the backfield before we were ready to block him). I pictured him blowing past me time after time and sacking the quarterback. The next moment, I thought, *You moron, just go to sleep. You'll deal with Howie when the time comes.*

It could be just as bad during the season. So often, if I knew I'd be facing one of those guys on Sunday, my guts got so twisted during our Wednesday morning game prep meeting that I had to step out of the room for a minute. The feeling was close to despair. Yet, as we went over our game plan over the next couple days, I'd always calm down and feel better. By Friday I'd be confident again. That's the kind of mental havoc the great players could create. Not that there was ever a chance to relax in the NFL. I learned quickly that if I underestimated any opponent, he was sure to ruin my day.

Those mental anxieties were just as prevalent, if not more so, when we played the Browns during my first eleven years in the league or the Falcons during the next three. People often ask me to name the toughest player I ever faced. My answer is Bruz. The main reason is that he was a great player, but for me there was added anticipation and pressure that came from playing against family. I always looked forward to it, but I also did not want that guy to beat me.

When I look back on my career, I also value the memories I have of so many great teammates, particularly the camaraderie we established on the offensive line. We depended on each other, performed in relative obscurity, and embraced our roles. I have good memories of every O-line guy I played with, going back to USC and even Arcadia. For me, the offensive line players and coaches epitomize what *team* is all about.

Sometimes, I'm asked not only to look back on my career but also to look ahead. I see a bright future for football. The game is as popular as ever. As always, there are improvements to be made and problems to work out. The devastating impact of concussions has been debated frequently in the media. I had only a couple of documented concussions during my career, though I had my bell rung several times. The culture back in the day was if you could play, you played, no questions asked. That's changing today, as it should, as more information about ways to make the game safer comes to light.

I understand why some guys look at the dangers and decide to retire early. But I've never tried to discourage my kids from playing. Yes, football is a sometimes violent sport with inherent risks. But we take a risk just getting out of bed and walking down the street. There's nothing like the opportunity to test your skills and will to win against the best in the world. For me and many other guys, the risk was worth it. It was a privilege to play the game.

I've played or coached football for most of my life. It's taught me about myself and about life and led to relationships and memories that I will always cherish. As much as the game means to me, however, my family means even more. They are my life.

I've said plenty—probably too much—about myself in this book. Now I want to add a few words about each of my kids and give them a chance to comment on what it means to be a Matthews.

Steven has always loved to read and is the most intellectual of our offspring. Though he played football growing up and is a passionate fan, he's applied that competitive Matthews spirit to more constructive pursuits. He recently finished law school, an impressive achievement, and intends to practice in the Houston area.

"One thing I appreciate a lot more today than I did growing up," Steven says, "is being part of a big family. When I was in high school, as the oldest, it was suffocating having all my younger siblings around me. Now, I think it's great to have so many brothers and sisters around. I have so many great memories of my family and extended family."

When the kids were young, Kevin was our little outdoorsman. He was always hunting snakes or squirrels and is still passionate about hunting today. He married his high school sweetheart, Amanda, and has two wonderful little boys, Weston and Sawyer. Yes, I'm a proud grandpa. As stated earlier, Kevin signed and played with the Titans in 2010. Then, in 2014, he signed a contract with the Carolina Panthers but injured his shoulder during the preseason and spent the year on injured reserve. He decided to move on from football and is now channeling his talent and energy into the real-estate business.

Kevin credits his determination to walk on at Texas A&M and earn a scholarship, as well as persevere through five years in the NFL, at least in part to our family's don't-quit philosophy: "That was instilled in us at a young age, that you put your mind to whatever you're doing and keep at it till it works out."

Now, ask any father who has girls, and you're almost sure to hear him say there's something special about that father-daughter relationship. Marilyn is certainly no exception for me. Carrie likes to tell the story of how I pulled aside Marilyn's boyfriend before they went off to college and said, "I just want to let you know, if I ever hear anything about my daughter that I don't want to hear, I am going to come up there and kick your rear end." I feel the same way about Gwenie. I just want to protect them every way that I can.

Marilyn enjoys watching and supporting the family's football exploits, but becoming a big-time athlete herself has never been a priority. For example, during a YMCA league basketball game when she was nine, while everyone else ran down the court she started doing cartwheels. Marilyn is an occupational therapy assistant at the Institute for Rehabilitation and Research (TIRR) Memorial Hermann in Houston, where she works with people dealing with brain injuries. She points to our family's love and support for each other as one of the foundations of being a Matthews. She also feels that she's learned a thing or two from her mom and dad, which is always gratifying for a father to hear.

"By watching how my parents lived their lives," she says, "we learned to respect all people, to treat others the way you want to be treated, and that everyone deserves a chance."

Jake was our first Texas-bred child. He'd been a quarterback since he began playing in Pee Wee football, but once he tried offensive tackle in high school he knew he'd found his sweet spot. He was an outstanding player at Elkins High and an All-American at Texas A&M. The one time I've had any alcohol since I quit drinking was in April 2014—I had a glass of champagne to celebrate Jake being drafted sixth overall, the highest ever for a Matthews, by the Atlanta Falcons. He's been their starting left tackle ever since and his NFL career is off to a great start.

"Our family is a pretty down-to-earth group," Jake says. "We usually don't say much and we work hard. And If we commit to some thing, we're not going to quit. That mindset almost goes without saying for the whole family."

Mikey is in some ways the opposite of me as a football player. Even when I first started coaching and Mikey was an eight-year-old, he showed a wild, vocal passion as a player. He'd run down the field yelling and screaming like a madman. I remember him taking guys out as a blocker, which was great except that it was during pregame warmups and they were on our team. He was a natural and knew it, to the point that he once basically told me that he knew as much about offensive line play as I did. He was nine years old at the time.

Recently, Mikey confessed to giving me a few difficult moments back then. "How'd you put up with me?" he said. "I must have been a pain to coach."

"Exactly," I said.

Mikey had an exceptional career at Texas A&M and was among the final roster cuts by the Cleveland Browns before the 2016 season. He has a great chance to join another team and carve out an NFL career.

"For me, it's a dream come true," Mikey says. "People ask if I feel extra pressure to live up to the Matthews family reputation, but we were always told we didn't have to play football, so I don't feel any pressure. I play the game because I love it and want to accomplish my own dreams."

Luke was christened "The Boy" by Kevin soon after he was born and the nickname has stuck—though at six feet four inches and 310 pounds, he doesn't look much like a boy anymore. When he was younger he loved to follow his brothers or me around. He would "help" Kevin and Mikey when they were taking care of cows for a Future Farmers of America show or run a gasser with me during my workouts. Today, he's still following in those footsteps. The coaches at Texas A&M must have liked what they saw in Kevin, Jake, and Mikey, because they offered Luke a football scholarship in 2015. He won't graduate from high school until 2018.

Like many of his siblings, Luke also points to our family's closeness as a reason for whatever success we've achieved. "Everyone's very caring," he says. "We support each other's decisions and are happy to be together. It's a tight-knit group."

Gwenie would agree. When she's with the family, giving and receiving hugs, you can tell there's no place she'd rather be. I've loved watching her siblings grow up, take on new responsibilities, and chase their dreams, but it's a blessing to know that even when Luke moves on, we'll still have Gwenie at home. No matter what happens with the weather, she is the daily sunshine in my life.

Since this is a football book, I'd be remiss if I didn't give the family's other NFL veterans a chance to comment as well on what's allowed so many of us to pursue a career in the game.

You already know about Bruz. Today he's enjoying the California life, being a dad and grandfather, and attending games being played by the family's next generation. As far as any Matthews family secrets to success, he points to two things: "Number one is that we're blessed with bodies that can take a licking. It's allowed us to show up day in and day out." (Speaking of good genes, Carrie says she deserves credit for our kids' NFL success too. As evidence, she points to her nephew Troy Niklas, who's been a tight end with the Arizona Cardinals since 2014. I have to admit that she's probably right.)

"And then, to a degree," Bruz adds, "we want to be the best. I give my dad credit for that. He always told us, 'Look, if you're going to do something, do it to the best of your ability. Why not be the best at it?'"

Bruz's son Clay III—we call him "Little Clay"—is the best known of the current Matthews players in the NFL. After walking on at USC, he became one of the team's top players and has since found tremendous success as an outside linebacker with the Packers. He has a motor that never seems to stop running, on the field and off. He and his wife, Casey, have a son named—naturally—Clay IV.

Clay agrees with his dad that genetics and a drive to be the best have fueled the Matthews NFL legacy. The longer he plays, he says, the more meaningful that becomes.

"When you're younger you tend to take it all for granted," Clay says. "But the older you get, the more you look at families with a legacy, like the Mannings. Then you look at our family and all the statistics, the games and years played, the Pro Bowls. To do that generation after generation—that is something special, something we take a lot of pride in."

You might wonder if Clay wants his son to continue the legacy.

"There won't be any pressure to play," he says. "Hopefully, he'll be a surgeon or something where he can use his brain rather than hitting his head against people. But if he's so inclined to pick up a football and get after it? Absolutely, I'm going to encourage him and help him develop the tools he needs."

The original Casey in the family is Clay's younger brother. He and his wife, Alyssa, live in California and have a son, Braylon. After helping lead Oregon to the national championship game following the 2010 season, Casey played linebacker for four years with the Philadelphia Eagles, which included eleven starts in 2014. A hip injury forced him to spend 2015 on injured reserve with the Minnesota Vikings.

Though Casey always loved the game, it wasn't until his brother was drafted by the Packers that the NFL felt like an attainable dream. "When I was in college and saw that," Casey says, "and I knew that the next step was the pros, that's when I changed my focus, hunkered down, and started pushing myself as hard as I could."

Maybe part of being a Matthews means being just plain stubborn.

"I think it's how we were raised, starting with my great-grandpa, Matty Matthews," Casey says. "It's been passed down to us. We've got this stubborn mentality—whatever we want, we're going to work as hard as we can to get it."

I believe that, as a group, the Matthews family has worked hard to build a loving, supportive family. It doesn't happen as often as it used to, but all the cousins talk about how much they enjoy our family gatherings. When they were younger, that meant renting beach houses in Charleston or staying on our property near Houston for Easter. Those Easter celebrations were major productions that included an Easter basket hunt. One year, Carrie hollowed out ten empty pizza box cartons—we did put away a lot of food—and hid a basket inside. There was also hunting and fishing, as well as spirited egg-toss and basketball competitions. The main event for the kids, though, seemed to be roaming over our acreage on four-wheelers, go-carts, and dirt bikes, along with riding the tractors we used to haul trees and brush to create a massive bonfire. It was always a good time.

Today, it seems to be weddings that bring us all together, most recently when Little Clay and Casey tied the knot. The next day we were all in Bruz and Leslie's backyard, eating catered Mexican food and—what else?—competing. Mikey and Luke were probably facing off against Clay and Steven in a KanJam disc game while Bruz and I played hoops (I'm sure I must have won). It's what we do.

Bruz and I may no longer have the opportunity to square off against each other in the NFL, but the current generation still features an occasional round of Matthews vs. Matthews. In 2014, Jake's rookie year, the Packers hosted the Falcons at Lambeau Field. "It was exciting," Jake says. "It was my first Monday night game; it snowed in the first half. It was the perfect environment. And it was pretty cool to play against my cousin, someone I grew up with. I finally got to see how good he was."

Of course there was some mild trash talk between the cousins during the game. At one point after a play, the veteran decided to introduce the rookie to the NFL and gave him a shove. "He turned around real quick, then saw it was me," Clay says. "He got this smirk on his face. A few plays later, after they gashed us for a run, he shoved me in the back. That's the type of relationship we have—it's fun. It's all about competing."

Whether they're competing in the NFL or in the larger arena of life, I am so proud of each of my kids and extended family. They're all winners and all represent the family name with honor. They are my true legacy. I couldn't ask for more.

Today, I enjoy my life in the Houston area. Besides spending time with the family, I'm leading or helping lead three Bible studies, serving as a chair or cochair of Special Olympics and Fellowship of Christian Athletes golf tournaments, hosting a football camp for kids, and volunteering at a food bank. I'm grateful to have the time now to do those things.

I also still find ways to satisfy my competitive urges, whether it's a Taboo board game with my family or a doubles tennis match. But I'm living for more than that. Especially since I retired, I've become aware that God doesn't want me to sit on the sidelines. He's given me a platform to share with people about the hope that I have in Christ and I have a responsibility to use it. I recently joined a national speaker's bureau to facilitate that. I still get anxious about standing up and speaking in public, but I also realize that when I step out in faith and trust in God's power instead of my own, it's going to be okay.

I want to be more available to the Lord. He's been showing me that if I'm willing to get out of my comfort zone, He can use me in ways that will touch people's lives. It doesn't get more rewarding than that.

I don't know what my future holds, but I know that God has a plan for it. I can't wait.

I'm also so grateful that I get to share that future with Carrie. She is a gift from the Lord. Back in Canton, when I made my Hall of Fame speech, I looked at each member of the audience when I expressed my thanks for his or her contribution to my life. I was worried about letting my emotions get the best of me, but I held it together pretty well until I got to Carrie. When I looked at her, I nearly lost it. The words I said then still apply today: "She is the one thing that I cherish most on this earth. You are my best friend and I hate to think what life would be without you. As great as all the athletic awards and accolades have been, they do not compare to knowing and loving you. I thank God for you and I look forward to whatever He has in store for us next."

It's been a great journey and it's still going. I keep saying it because there's no other way to describe it: I've been blessed.

ACKNOWLEDGMENTS

IN 2007, AROUND THE TIME THAT I was named to the Hall of Fame, I was surprised by a statement from my financial advisor, Jay Branson: "You know, Bruce, you should write a book about your experiences and life. Then you should speak about them."

My response was less than total enthusiasm: "Are you out of your mind?"

Undaunted, Jay put me in touch with a speaker's bureau, which led me to an excellent literary agent named Frank Breeden. Frank also encouraged me to pursue a book.

I had no interest in writing a book. Who would want to read about me? But if people I respected thought it was a good idea, I figured I'd better pray about it. I also talked it through with Carrie. The consensus was that if the Lord was nudging me in the direction of a book, I'd better not stand in His way. As I've gotten past my anxiety over feeling I have nothing to say, I've sensed the Lord telling me, "You don't have to do any heavy lifting. I'm the one who's going to change lives. Just trust Me."

To my surprise, I've actually enjoyed the book experience. With that in mind, I have a few people to thank:

Jay Branson, for suggesting the idea and putting the wheels in motion.

Frank Breeden, for recognizing the potential of this project before I could see it and for your enthusiasm and professionalism every step of the way.

Jim Lund, for your ability to draw my story out of me and for making this process so easy for Carrie and me. As you know, I was reluctant to read those first few chapters, but once I realized it was a great read, I couldn't wait for the next one.

Lisa Stilwell and the entire team at Howard Books, for your commitment to, and enthusiasm for, this book and for inviting me into your publishing family.

Robbie Bohren in the Titans organization, for help with game stats, and Bob Green, for comments on the manuscript.

All the friends, teammates, coaches, opponents, pastors, mentors, and fans who have shared the journey with me, including those named in the book and those I didn't have room to mention. I wouldn't be here without your support.

My family. You guys mean everything to me. You're more than the NFL's First Family—you're my First Family. I love each one of you.

Lastly, my wife, Carrie. Your encouragement, feedback, wisdom, and love have blessed me throughout not just the process of writing this book, but every day we've been together. You make it all worthwhile.

ABOUT THE AUTHORS

BRUCE MATTHEWS is one of the greatest offensive linemen to ever play in the National Football League. He was selected to fourteen consecutive Pro Bowls, tied for the all-time record; holds the NFL record for games played by an offensive lineman (296); and is a member of the NFL Hall of Fame. During a nineteen-year career, he never missed a game due to injury. Bruce was named to the NFL Hall of Fame's All-Decade Team (1990s) and All-Time Team. Before playing professionally, he was an All-American at the University of Southern California. Today, he serves as chair or cochair of Special Olympics and Fellowship of Christian Athletes golf tournaments, hosts a youth football camp, and volunteers for charitable organizations. Bruce and his wife, Carrie, have seven children and live in Sugar Land, Texas.

JAMES LUND is an award-winning collaborator and editor, and the coauthor of *A Dangerous Faith* and *Danger Calling*. He works with bestselling authors and public figures such as Max Lucado, Tim Brown, George Foreman, Kathy Ireland, and Jim Daly. Three of his projects earned the Evangelical Christian Publishers Association Gold Medallion Award. Visit his website at www.jameslundbooks.com.